Collins
LAKEL
FELLRANGER

SOUTHERN FELLS

MARK RICHARDS

HarperCollinsPublishers Ltd.
77-85 Fulham Palace Road
London
W6 8JB

The Collins website address is:
www.collins.co.uk

Collins is a registered trademark of
HarperCollinsPublishers Ltd.

First published in 2005

10 09 08 07 06 05

10 9 8 7 6 5 4 3 2 1

A catalogue record for this book is available from the British Library.

ISBN 0 00 711367 6

Colour reproduction by Colourscan, Singapore
Printed and bound in Singapore

(cover) Coniston Water and the Old Man from Great How Crags
(title page) White Combe from Blackcombe Screes

CONTENTS

Key to maps and diagrams   GRID NORTH IS TOP OF EVERY MAP

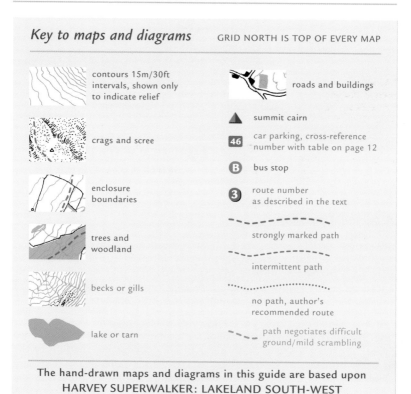

contours 15m/30ft intervals, shown only to indicate relief

crags and scree

enclosure boundaries

trees and woodland

becks or gills

lake or tarn

roads and buildings

summit cairn

46 car parking, cross-reference number with table on page 12

B bus stop

3 route number as described in the text

- - - - - - - strongly marked path

- - - - - - - intermittent path

.... no path, author's recommended route

- - - - path negotiates difficult ground/mild scrambling

The hand-drawn maps and diagrams in this guide are based upon
HARVEY SUPERWALKER: LAKELAND SOUTH-WEST

LAKELAND FELLRANGER

CALDBECK

COCKERMOUTH

Northern Fells

PENRITH

KESWICK

North-Western Fells

Central Fells

Near Eastern Fells

Western Fells

EGREMONT

Far Eastern Fells

Mid-Western Fells

AMBLESIDE

Southern Fells

KENDAL

Eight title divisions of the English Lake District

BROUGHTON-IN-FURNESS

A personal passion

My earliest memories of Lakeland came through studying artistic essays and books of the picturesque that my mother had acquired. They portrayed the romance of a majestic landscape that had formed the backdrop to her youth. Born in north Lancashire, she naturally knew of Lakeland as a special place, though she had little opportunity to visit.

At a similar time, through the tales of Black Bob, the *Dandy* wonder dog, comic strip stories of a shepherd's adventures on the hills above Selkirk, I gained a love of both pen and ink drawing and the hills of the Scottish Borders, all distantly set in a romantic land of my own very youthful dreams. For I was born in rural west Oxfordshire and the magic that my mother clung to was becoming increasingly real to me.

Holidays were always allied to my parents' roots. My father's Cornish ancestry gave me early seaside trips to that wonderful coastline and, as my teenage years unfolded, a regular busman's holiday to a fell farm on Lord Shuttleworth's Leck Hall estate gave me the hands-on feel and flavour of rough fell country. My first fragmentary taste of what Lakeland itself was all about came, when I was twelve years old, on a day-trip to Ambleside and Great Langdale, when I remember purchasing *The Southern Fells*, Book Four of Alfred Wainwright's *A Pictorial Guide to the Lakeland Fells*. That book was periodically perused as my formative life as a young farmer kept my attention firmly on the needs of a 150-acre farm of cattle and corn. Socially I revelled in the activities of the Young Farmers' movement. I remember an exchange with the Alnwick club gave me a chance to climb the Cheviot in smooth-soled leather shoes, my first real fell climb. After masterminding two ploughing marathons – 100, then 200 acres turned from stubble to tilth in 24 hours – in my early twenties I sought new adventures. I joined the Gloucestershire Mountaineering Club and got to grips with Snowdonia, Scotland and yes, at long last, the Lakeland Fells. Rock climbing and long days in all weathers ridge walking put me in touch with the thrill of high places.

That first Wainwright guide focused my mind on a love of wild places, Lakeland in particular. Quickly I now acquired the remainder of the series and, feeling far removed from the beauty of it all, I took to drawing from my own black and white photographs, mimicking AW. Within a year of joining the Mountaineering Club I had become a firm friend of the legend himself, spending regular weekends at Kendal Green, joining him on his original exploration of the *Coast to Coast Walk*, *The Outlying Fells (see page 228 for my one moment of recognition)*, *Westmorland Heritage* and supplying numerous photographs of Scottish mountains he was unable to reach for his *Scottish Mountain Drawings* series. As my walking progressed and his faltered, so my trips to Kendal became fewer. Marriage, a family and farming brought responsibilities so time constraints deflected my attention from AW and the Lakeland I loved.

I remained in farming until almost forty, during which time I had several walking guides published. AW nurtured my first title, a very pictorial map-guide to the Cotswold Way back in 1973. This was followed by guides to the North Cornwall Coast, Offa's Dyke Path, a three-part exploration of the Peak District National Park and Hadrian's Wall, as well as many small guides and articles, including a happy sequence of *Out of the Way* pieces for *The Countryman*, a journal I had known from childhood, published on my doorstep. All along gnawing at the back of my mind was the sense that some day I should prepare my own complete survey of the Lakeland Fells. Having edited a little magazine, *Walking Wales,* for one year, I found I could ignore it no longer and, with the support and encouragement of HarperCollins, to whom I will be forever grateful, I moved to Cumbria to begin *Lakeland Fellranger*.

The Bell and Wetherlam from the Walna Scar Road fell-gate

From fireside to fellside

Packaging the fells into neat fellwalking areas is not a hard and exact science but the forces of nature are to be congratulated on giving some semblance of order to the high ridges. The one grey area comes south and east of the Scafells where a wild tangle of upland merges with the Coniston Fells. Here the Romans have come to our aid, in laying their military road from Ambleside to Ravenglass over the high passes of Wrynose and Hardknott - a deliciously juicy route adored by motorised travellers to this day. Wainwright found it expedient to combine the fells south of Borrowdale with the higher fells of this southern group and turn a blind eye to the superb tramping to be found down the Duddon to Black Combe. Hence the doyen of the fellwalking tradition denied the existence of a Mid-Western group altogether! The matter is now resolved, there *are* eight divisions of the Lakeland fells. However, even this author is loath to concede that there might yet even be nine divisions! While the A6 inserts a firm end to affairs for the purposes of this series, the actual farthest frontier of the Far Eastern Fells surely is the Eden/Ure watershed at the head of Mallerstang. The Howgills and Wild Boar are hybrid Pennine/Lakeland, yet sustained classic fellwalking country to be enjoyed and venerated accordingly.

  So this guide is a new compendium, bringing together a happy compilation of twenty-three fells: an intriguing mix of the wildly popular Coniston Old Man and Wetherlam, with the wild and solitary Yoadcastle and Black Combe. Hitherto unceremoniously divorced, all are explored upon trailworthy routes for discerning fellwalkers that give you every cause to take a new look and break away from the familiar areas of central Lakeland.

How two seasons can differ. During 2003 my research into the Mid-Western Fells was blessed with an unbroken chain of gorgeous days. I could leave my north Pennine home and drive to Langdale or Borrowdale in complete and utter confidence that I would get a full day's walking and wield my camera with abandon. I was lulled into a false sense of security, 2004 has treated me to relentless rains, grey cloud hanging over the district month after month. Publishing deadlines rearing like the Great Wall of China to a Mongol tribesman. To quote Vicky Slowe, curator of the Ruskin Museum, 'It's been a fantastically wet year!'

During the course of the preparation of this guide I was asked by *Country Walking* magazine to nominate my top ten viewpoints in the Lake District. A daunting task at the best of times, but why only the ten! I needed to do this before even setting foot on Black Fell, Harter Fell and Wallowbarrow Crag, each possessing their own brand of exquisite Lakeland fell outlook. Even Caw, Stickle Pike, Buckbarrow and far-flung Black Combe all merit scenic pride in this book.

In *Mid-Western Fells* I mentioned the work of the Upland Path Landscape Restoration Project (UPLRP) pitching the most seriously damaged fell paths. The process has been a great learning curve, the more recent pitching is superb, ensuring a flat footfall where possible, easy to use in ascent and descent. However, invariably these trails are not rights-of-way and therefore beyond the statutory responsibility of the highway authority. The National Park Authority, National Trust and English Nature have worked in partnership to make good the hill paths, with additional financial support from the Friends of the Lake District and the whole effort has been made possible by third-part match funding from the Heritage Lottery Fund. But when this vital cash injection ends in 2006 much work will remain to be done, especially pre-emptive repair to prevent paths from washing out.

The Lake District Tourism & Conservation Partnership also contributes significantly to this work, but with a metre of path costing up to £100 there is every good reason to cultivate the involvement of fellwalkers in a cause that must be dear to their hearts... and soles! UPLRP have created a website for this purpose –www.fixthefells.co.uk – encouraging walkers to make donations. Clearly the occasional donation is welcome, but as yet this is still only a tiny injection. Perhaps it needs to become the culture for fellwalkers to make small regular donations. Creative thinking is needed.

One thought would be to nurture the natural collecting habit of many hillgoers. In this guide I have set out three pages for readers to mark up the fells they climb. Why not take that another step? Create a passport stamping system for dedicated fellwalkers to amass their tally of fells, the

price of the card could be a further contribution to the Fixthefells fund *(also read page 240)*.

In May 2005 Cumbria sees the implementation of the Countryside and Rights of Way Act, from which time most rough open country will become conditionally accessible. The so-called 'right to roam' legislation is in truth something of a sledge-hammer to crack a nut. Quite the majority of fellwalkers only feel at ease when striding upon a clear path, especially one that has a time-honoured sense of purpose. The roving instinct, a broad-brush freedom to randomly explore trackless country appeals to a narrower band of walkers. I love the liberty of exploring open country with a map, but being wedded to the preparation of practical guides, always have an eye on sensible routes that give the security guidebook-users expect. This guide shows only a few such 'roaming' routes. Future editions will give more expression, as it becomes opportune and appropriate to fix lines on a map. Harmonising with the start of Open Access, Ordnance Survey are releasing new *Explorer* maps with the precise areas defined in orange tint. This guide would be falling short if the mantra of Open Access was not stressed – **Respect, Protect and Enjoy,** for liberty brings responsibilities. As wanderers we acknowledge that the land has value, not just confined to its ownership, and we should know the part we can play in its sustaining care.

This greater access is seen by the soon-to-be-subsumed Countryside Agency as the catalyst for a change in long-established rambling routes. Open Access brings new opportunities for people to grasp greater outdoor horizons, encouraging a perfect coalescence of natural heritage and people.

The Scafells and Coniston group from Duddon Estuary Youth Hostel

Yew Tree Farm backed by the sunlit eastern slopes of Wetherlam

Being constantly alive to, and aware of, the lurking dangers of walking in the high fell country is an imperative for everyone especially those coming new to the thrills and wish to avoid the spills! The National Park Authority provides practical and up-to-date advice, from daily weather checks to guided walks for absolute beginners. As a first recourse, obtain a copy of its leaflet 'Safety on the Fells' and consult their website : www.lake-district.gov.uk.

The Authority has prepared a short advisory note for conscientious fellwalkers :

Place your feet thoughtfully; every single footstep causes wear and tear on the environment. The slow-growing plants that can survive on mountains are particularly vulnerable.

Keep to the path surface; do not walk along the vegetation at the edge of the path.

Do not build or add to cairns – paths need stones more than cairns.

Do not take shortcuts – water will soon follow your tracks and an erosion scar will develop.

Remember, there may be only one of you, but there are another 12 million pairs of feet treading Lake District paths every year.

Tarn on Holme Fell

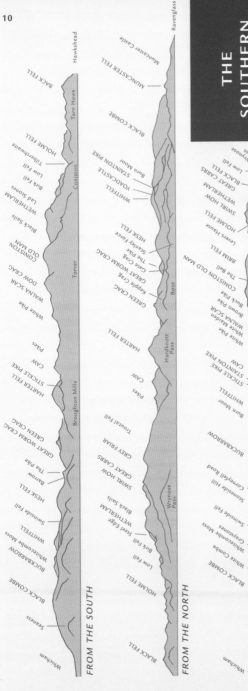

THE SOUTHERN FELLS

four graphic projections of the range

FROM THE SOUTH

FROM THE NORTH

FROM THE EAST

FROM THE WEST

FELL MOSAIC

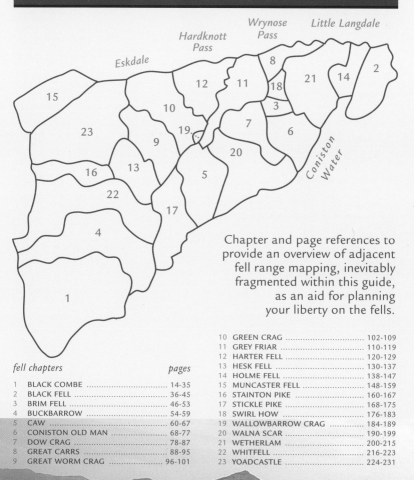

Wrynose Pass

Little Langdale

Hardknott Pass

Eskdale

Coniston Water

Chapter and page references to provide an overview of adjacent fell range mapping, inevitably fragmented within this guide, as an aid for planning your liberty on the fells.

Caw from Baskell Farm

STARTING POINTS

	LOCATION	GRID REFERENCE	PARKING	BUS STOP
1	Hardknott Pass	228 015		
2	Jubilee Bridge	213 012	P	
3	Woolpack Inn	190 101	P	
4	Stanley Ghyll	171 003	P	
5	Birkerfell Road (*Devoke Water track-end*)	171 977		
6	Birkerfell Road (*Woodend Bridge*)	328 047		
7	Eskdale Green	146 986	P	
8	Brantrake	113 952		
9	Ravenglass	146 986	P	
10	Dyke	113 952		
11	Corneyfell Road (*Fell Lane*)	116 938		
12	Corneyfell Road (*Buckbarrow Bridge*)	134 904		
13	Corneyfell Road (*road summit*)	896 150		
14	Bootle	107 884		
15	Whitbeck	118 839		*
16	Whicham Church	135 826	P	*
17	Beckside	153 847		*
18	Hallthwaites	178 856		
19	Cragg Hall	181 877		
20	Brackenthwaite	178 922		
21	Bobbinmill Bridge	190 926		
22	Ulpha	199 919		
23	Kiln Bank Cross	214 933		
24	Broughton Mills	223 907		
25	Water Yeat (*forest gate*)	238 928		
26	Hummer Lane	268 934		
27	Torver (*church hall*)	285 944	P	
28	Walna Scar Road (*fell-gate*)	288 971	P	
29	Coniston (*Lake Road*)	307 973	P	*
30	Tilberthwaite	305 010	P	
31	Hodge Close	315 016	P	
32	Oxen Fell (*High Cross*)	328 017		
33	Tom Gill	186 085	P	
34	Tarn Hows (*NT*)	326 996	P	
35	High Cross	333 985	P	*
36	Silverthwaite	341 037	P	*
37	Little Langdale	319 033		
38	Cathedral Quarry	315 028		
39	Castle How	296 032		
40	Wrynose Pass	277 027		
41	Wrynose Bottom	265 023		
42	Cockley Beck Bridge	246 016		
43	Birks Bridge	235 995	P	
44	Troutal	235 988		
45	Fickle Steps	231 974		
46	Seathwaite	229 963		

P - formal car parking facilities (some with coin meters) otherwise informal verge or lay-by parking.
* - serviced bus stop close by. Public transport to this quarter of Lakeland is less effective as a means of walk planning. There is a coastal railway service which gives scope for access to Black Combe via Silecroft station, and, Buckbarrow and Whitfell via Bootle station, while Stagecoach service X6 also runs up the A595 from Barrow to Whitehaven. Regular buses do not penetrate the Duddon valley or Eskdale, though service 6 is useful. This runs from Whitehaven via Egremont to Ravenglass, thereby making a link with L'aal Ratty. The most useful bus route is the Coniston Rambler service 505 from Windermere to Coniston via Hawkshead. Coniston is also connected with Ulverston by service X12, via Torver. For current advice : **TRAVELINE** public transport info 0870 608 2 608

THE SOUTHERN FELLS

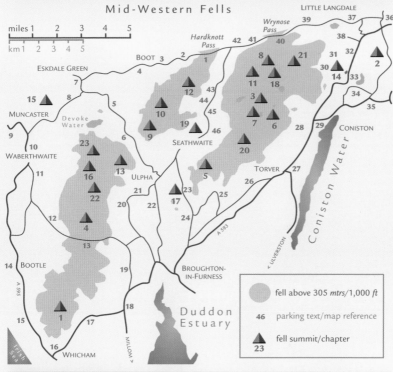

Mid-Western Fells

LITTLE LANGDALE

miles 1 2 3 4 5

km 1 2 3 4 5

Wrynose Pass

Hardknott Pass

BOOT

ESKDALE GREEN

MUNCASTER

Devoke Water

WABERTHWAITE

ULPHA

SEATHWAITE

TORVER

CONISTON

Coniston Water

BOOTLE

BROUGHTON-IN-FURNESS

Duddon Estuary

Irish Sea

WHICHAM

MILLOM

ULVERSTON

A 593

A 595

● fell above 305 *mtrs*/1,000 *ft*

46 parking text/map reference

▲ fell summit/chapter
23

Upper Eskdale from the lower slopes of Harter Fell

BLACK COMBE

In embracing the West Cumbrian seaboard, from Ravenglass down to the Whicham valley, the National Park gathers both a fascinating shore and takes into the fold one fine fell massif. Black Combe will forever draw admiration from those who live and work in its near shadow. It has a presence that deludes the innocent into thinking it to be greater than the mighty Scafells. What it lacks in volcanicity it more than makes up for in solid form. It rests squat, resolute and reassuring, a cornerstone bulwark marking the fells' beginning and end.

 For more than fifty years Harry Griffin wrote with huge affection on the craggy heights of central Lakeland, a Barrow man, Black Combe was his parochial favourite, a sentiment shared by Norman Nicholson from across the Duddon estuary in Millom. William Wordsworth was moved to venture to its summit which elicited profound elation on the view, an emotion shared by Wainwright. AW concluded that this 'landmark' fell 'was made to be climbed'. Remote from regular fellwalking territory, it deserves more than a perfunctory inspection. Indeed, many make forays to the top, for the view of land and sea is quite exceptional and infinitely variable through the time and tide.

600 *metres*   1,970 *feet*

Black Combe brooding in the morning light from Duddon estuary Youth Hostel

Surveyed from the summit, the working world of south and west Cumbria displays an historic industrial scene from the Walney shipyards and old Millom ironworks, swinging north beyond the Calder Hall /Windscale/Sellafield complex to the headland of St Bees shielding the former marine coalfields of Workington and Whitehaven. Black Combe is reminiscent of the Howgills, rounded ridges notably fall to west and south, though the moorland form of the northern slopes is more Pennine in character. Whitecombe Beck etches deep into the southern slopes, giving the fell its greatest dramatic statement; the splintered screes falling into eastern hollows, those nearest the summit more prone to shadow, give rise to the fell-name.

Most visitors climb the fell by the Whicham path. However the fell's Christmas pudding shape means that anyone seeking to make a circular outing invariably chooses to advance up the Whitecombe Beck valley, wending to its head, then leaving the summit by one or other of the ridges flanking Blackcombe Screes. Few walkers climb from Bootle, though there is a steady grassy way, useful in creating a circular outing beginning from Whitbeck. There is but one northern and one eastern approach, of value in grand traverses but awkward when it comes to making a tidy circuit. Walkers who find ancient sites riveting should make a point of visiting Sunkenkirk stone circle, though at present the natural ridge above Swinside Farm is not readily accessible (delicate ridge-top wall with need of a ladder-stile).

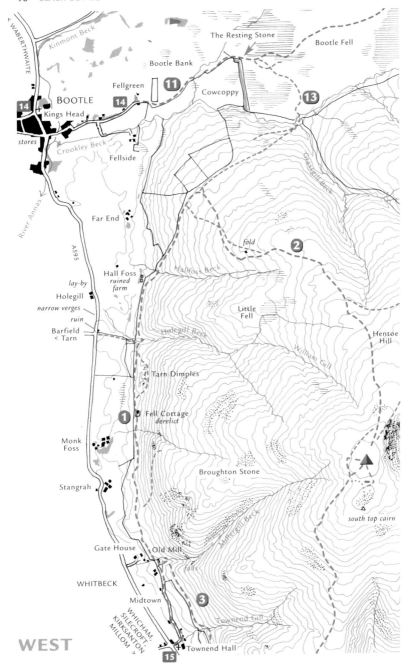

< WABERTHWAITE

Kinmont Beck

The Resting Stone

Bootle Fell

Bootle Bank

Fellgreen

11

Cowcoppy

13

BOOTLE

14

14

Kings Head

stores

Crookley Beck

Fellside

Grassgill Beck

Far End

fold

2

River Annas

Halfoss Beck

A595

Little
Fell

Hall Foss
*ruined
farm*

lay-by

Holegill

Hentoe
Hill

narrow verges

ruin

Holegill Beck

Witham Gill

Barfield
< Tarn

Tarn Dimples

1

Fell Cottage
derelict

Monk
Foss

Broughton Stone

Stangrah

Millergill Beck

south top cairn

Gate House

Old Mill

falls

WHITBECK

Midtown

3

WHICHAM
SILECROFT
KIRKSANTON
MILLOM >

Townend Gill

WEST

15

Townend Hall

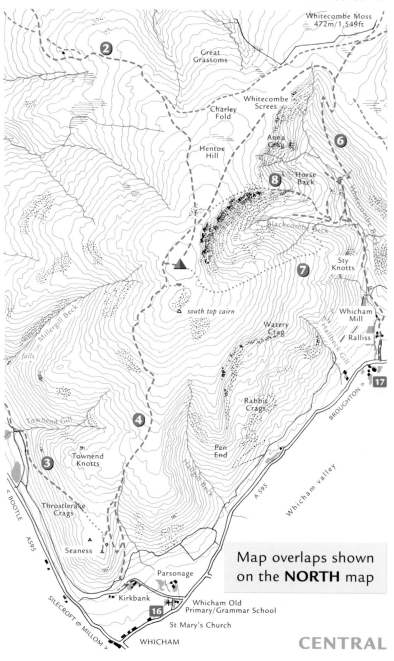

Whitecombe Moss
472m/1,549ft

Great
Grassoms

②

Charley
Fold

Whitecombe
Screes

Anna
Crag

⑥

Hentoe
Hill

⑧

Horse
Back

Blackcombe Beck

Whitecombe Beck

Sty
Knotts

⑦

south top cairn

Whicham
Mill

Ralliss

Watery
Crag

Millergill Beck

falls

Halbeck Gill

17

Townend Gill

Rabbit
Crags

BROUGHTON >

④

Townend
Knotts

Pen
End

③

Halfell Beck

A 595

Whicham valley

Throstlerake
Crags

Seaness

Parsonage

Map overlaps shown
on the **NORTH** map

Kirkbank

16

Whicham Old
Primary/Grammar School

< BOOTLE

A595

SILECROFT & MILLOM >

St Mary's Church

WHICHAM

CENTRAL

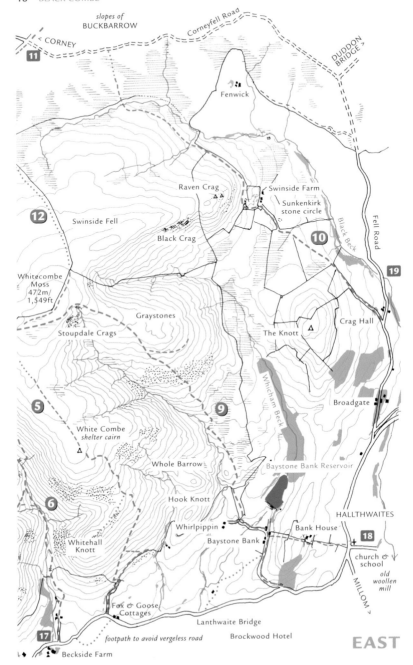

slopes of BUCKBARROW

Corneyfell Road

< CORNEY

DUDDON BRIDGE >

11

Fenwick

Raven Crag

Swinside Farm

Sunkenkirk stone circle

12

Swinside Fell

Black Crag

10

Black Beck

Fell Road

19

Whitecombe Moss 472m/ 1,549ft

Graystones

Crag Hall

Stoupdale Crags

The Knott

5

9

Whicham Beck

Broadgate

White Combe *shelter cairn*

Whole Barrow

Baystone Bank Reservoir

6

Hook Knott

HALLTHWAITES

Whitehall Knott

Whirlpippin

Baystone Bank

Bank House

18

church & school

old woollen mill

MILLOM >

Fox & Goose Cottages

17

footpath to avoid vergeless road

Lanthwaite Bridge

Brockwood Hotel

EAST

Beckside Farm

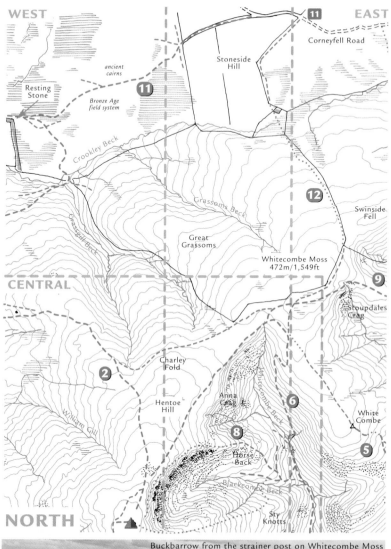

WEST

EAST

Corneyfell Road

Stoneside
Hill

11

ancient
cairns

11

Resting
Stone

Bronze Age
field system

Crookley Beck

Grassoms Beck

12

Swinside
Fell

Grassgill Beck

Great
Grassoms

Whitecombe Moss
472m/1,549ft

CENTRAL

9

Stoupdales
Crag

2

Charley
Fold

William Gill

Hentoe
Hill

Anna
Crag

Whitecombe Beck

6

White
Combe

8

5

Horse
Back

Blackcombe Beck

NORTH

Sty
Knotts

Buckbarrow from the strainer post on Whitecombe Moss

The preceding four map pages show the extent of Black Combe's fell territory, some 20 sq miles of, for many fellwalkers, virgin countryside. It is strange that so distinguished a fell should have no dedicated car park, though it has one public transport plus, railway stations comparatively close to its foot at Silecroft and Bootle and, importantly, very regular services along the Cumbrian Coast Line.

Zermatt is to the Matterhorn, what Coniston and Millom are respectively to the Old Man and Black Combe. Millom's man of letters Norman Nicholson had the fell very much in his sights, just as the author did during the preparation of this guide. Operating many miles from my home, the town proved a good base for creative expeditions. Rekindling my affection for youth hostelling, I took special pleasure in the Duddon estuary Hostel, which is especially well situated for considering Black Combe *(see images on pages 8 and 15, taken from the shore in front of the hostel enclosure)*.

The southern aspect from Kirksanton, with the railway and Brocklebanks old brewery

ASCENT *from Whitbeck*

Traffic shuttling along the A595 pays little heed to the charming hamlet of Whitbeck but walkers intent on a satisfying circuit of Black Combe may consider it a fine spot to stop. The loop is effected by using the Seaness and Bootle paths. The old road forms a useful lay-by in front of the church. **1** For simplicity and gentler walking the recommended route

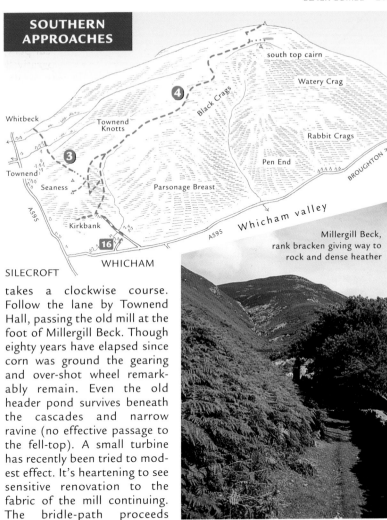

SOUTHERN APPROACHES

south top cairn

Watery Crag

4

Black Crags

Whitbeck

Townend Knotts

Rabbit Crags

3

Pen End

BROUGHTON ➤

Townend

Seaness

Parsonage Breast

A595

Kirkbank

16

Whicham valley

A595

Millergill Beck, rank bracken giving way to rock and dense heather

WHICHAM

SILECROFT

takes a clockwise course. Follow the lane by Townend Hall, passing the old mill at the foot of Millergill Beck. Though eighty years have elapsed since corn was ground the gearing and over-shot wheel remarkably remain. Even the old header pond survives beneath the cascades and narrow ravine (no effective passage to the fell-top). A small turbine has recently been tried to modest effect. It's heartening to see sensitive renovation to the fabric of the mill continuing. The bridle-path proceeds northbound initially with the intake wall close left, then across an undulating section, a clear way firmly striking through the dense bracken. There is a hint of a shepherd's path veering right at the first rise, climbing onto a natural shelf of the near ridge, potentially a good direct line of ascent or descent – route not tested. However, the circuit keeps faith with the lower path, passing the derelict Fell Cottage and a curious rigg feature with an even more intriguing name, Tarn Dimples. Just before the path fords Holegill Beck a footpath enters from the field-gate left. **2** This path begins at a gate off the busy A595 opposite the Barfield Tarn lane – a lay-by exists 460 metres

Rest is rust...   Rust In Peace

north, opposite Holegill Farm, though the verges are mean and the traffic even meaner! The path traverses the cattle pasture and via successive gates to the open fell at the ford. Go left over the ford, notice the hay-turner *(left)*. It must be forty years since it did June duty in the neighbouring hay meadows. Made of sterling iron it will last many a year yet. The ruinous Hall Foss can be seen over the wall left as the path next fords Hallfoss Beck and begins to rise beside the wall, then fence, onto the fell. Go right up the ridge as the ground levels opposite a gate in the intake wall. Route **13** from Bootle joins at this

point. The main ascending path winds up the shallow ridge eastward, mounting above a ruined fold and all too briefly through heather, onto Hentoe Hill. A lovely old shepherd's path breaks left across the northern slopes by the ruined square Charley Fold, enabling the full sweep of Whitecombe and Blackcombe Screes to be embraced in an exaggerated ascent. **3** The

A hazy Isle of Man from the Bootle path

alternative start turns immediately before the mill. Rise up the garden edge almost to the pond to veer right on a clear path above the enclosure wall. Ford Townend Gill, continue beside the fence on a firm farm track that duly angles up the scarp slope, petering out on the fell shoulder as a quad-bike track dwindles to a sheep trod on Seaness. Visit the first cairn, but the southernmost cairn has the loveliest view down the coastal margin to the wind cluster adjacent to Haverigg prison. The luckless inmates must hate the overbearing blades, which have a certain serenity from this range. Bear left regaining a clear path to join the popular path rising north from Kirkbank.

ASCENT *from Whicham*

4 This is the way of the many, stories of multiple ascents abound, sunrise and sunset treks too, it's the people's way without question. Begin from the church car park. There is a lay-by just before the turn into the church should a service be pending. Slip through between the old school and the church to join the byway beyond. Go left, rising behind

Kirkbank, the road becoming a track. Find a gate/stile after a recess gaining access to the open fell. Ascend the shallow combe merging with the Seaness path. A steady plod on firm turf ensures a happy mood is maintained. Coming above the second western re-entrant, the Millergill Beck valley, take the opportunity of breaking right to the tarn, veering back south over stony ground to reach the plump cairn on the south top, the

St Mary's Church, Whicham

perfect bird's eye view over the Millom and Barrow district. Backtrack to the fell summit, from where the prospect of Lakeland will tantalise.

Like a maritime daymark beacon the south cairn dominates the southern skyline

ASCENT *from Beckside*

The Whitecombe Beck valley gets right to the dark heart of the fell and not surprisingly offers the most impressive routes. Rather more surprising that so few walkers appear to take advantage of this fantastic arena. 5 Horse-shoe ridge walks are especially delectable and this valley-rimming ridge makes the perfect high way. From the generous lay-by close to Beckside Farm head east, taking full advantage of the field path, newly

White Combe from the brink of Blackcombe Screes

Northeast into the heart of Lakeland from Blackcombe Screes

equipped with hand-gates via Cross Bank, avoiding the vergeless main road. Regaining the road, enter the leafy footpath lane from a gate at the bend above Fox & Goose Cottages. The lane leads to a gate emerging onto the bracken slope of Whitehall Knott. Go up left, then diagonally across the slope on a grooved track mounting onto the northern shoulder. The short ridge of Whitehall Knott deserves a visit. It's a fine spot to peruse the Whicham valley and consider the fat ridge of Sty Knotts climbing to the top of Black Combe. Continuing by stunted gorse shrubs, the path gleefully fends off the bracken, being a drove-way. The ridge-end summit of White Combe is not the path's destiny, so watch to break left, latterly pathless, and still steep. The shelter cairn is a fine place to halt and delve into the rucksack for a bite to eat, while the great scoured hillsides of Black and Whitecombe Screes focus the attention.

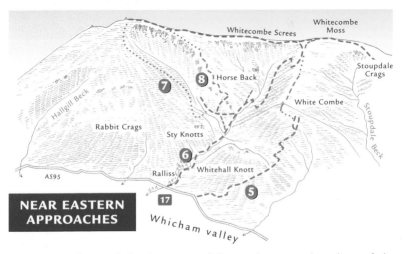

A narrow ridge path leads purposefully northwestward, only to fade approaching the junction with the valley-head path.

6 This path stems from the foot of the valley. Follow the gated lane direct from the main road at Beckside. Pass the old farmhouse of Ralliss, keeping right to avoid the immediate environs of Whicham Mill. As woodland ends a gate leads into the combe's inner sanctuary. The path skips over a plank footbridge, keeping to the west side of the beck until an obvious switch right over a broader plank footbridge. The path switches left, setting sights on climbing up the valley-head slope, latterly zig-zagging to curve naturally around the rim to complete the ascent in a southwesterly direction over easy ground.

Two ridges embrace Blackcombe Screes; Horse Bank **8** is the better climb, Styknotts **7** a preferred descent. To embark on either, watch left after fording the Blackcombe Gill, joining the first path keeping above

The meat and matter of Black Combe from White Combe

the north bank. Sty Knotts has little form, so the only advice is to hold with the clear path into the combe until a likely line is deduced, avoiding the worst of the bracken in climbing south then west with not the slightest sign of a path. The Horse Back ridge by contrast has a certain clientele, a path is faintly evident mounting above a small fenced area. As the ridge narrows the path threads up through rocks and climbs impressively in steps. Exciting situations abound.

White Combe and the pastoral Whicham valley from above Po House

Shelter created from an ancient cairn on the summit of White Combe

ASCENT *from Hallthwaites*

9 Approaches from the east have traditionally drawn up the Graystones ridge from the vicinity of Baystone Bank Reservoir. Car parking for anglers at the farm might, upon request of the tenant, extend to walkers. Guests at Brockwood Hotel have the best option – simply to follow the footpath from Lanthwaite Bridge. Otherwise walkers are obliged to begin at Hallthwaites, traversing the intermediate ridge on a footpath served by ladder-stiles via Bank House (hand-gate in tangled dip). The view from above Baystone Bank Farm is a delight. Joining the farm roadway at a stile, go right. In passing notice the farmhouse and a curious animal motif set high upon the wall. Is it a boar or badger?

Follow the lane as towards Whirlpippin. Short of the cottage, find a footpath signed right. Go through the gate and a brief lane opening into a pasture, the invisible path keeping close company with the left-hand wall. Latterly, dip, cross a

White Combe from Baystone Bank Reservoir

ditch and subsequent ladder-stile onto the open fell. For all its best endeavours bracken fails to subsume the path; slip over the wave-like knoll of Force Knott and keep order with Stoupdale Beck, always on the bank-top to the east. Marshy ground makes soft going until firmer ground eventually arrives and the path rises purposefully onto the western slope of Graystones. The facing fellside, known as Leadmine Breast, is a reminder of small-scale prospecting; similar delving in the Whitecombe Beck valley won copper ore. The path passes by gorse rising onto the ridge high above Stoupdale. Stoups were a form of Cumbrian stone gateposts, perhaps the name refers to a source of such stone. At the dale head a small broken slope bears the ambitious name Stoupdale Crags. The path skirts head-stream gullies; enjoy the fine view down the valley before heading over Whitecombe Moss peaty plateau slightly south of west to meet the path climbing out of the Whitecombe Beck valley. In mist a fence provides a limit on the north side of the table-top.

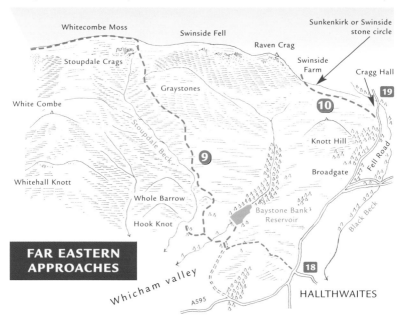

Sunkenkirk *from Cragg Hall*

The most easterly ridge on the Black Combe massif, Swinside Fell, has no tradition of access, despite the presence of cairns on the skyline of Raven Crag. So while Open Access will eventually bring freedoms even here, the lack of an adequate ladder-stile crossing the ridge-top wall above Raven Crag presently rules out any approach route to Black Combe along this narrow moorland ridge. **10** However, there is a good reason to

Swinside stone circle, folk-name Sunkenkirk, backed by Lath Rigg

consider tracing the bridle lane and open trackway from the vicinity of Cragg Hall towards Swinside Farm, for, located close to the farm buildings is a Bronze Age stone circle, composed of some fifty-five stones – I'll leave it to you to count, everyone comes up with a different number. The old name Sunkenkirk shows awareness of its ceremonial origins, though there is no hint of a ditch. Did 'sunken' mean drooped, likening the stones to a religious gathering in circular procession? There is no sign of rock art, though the centuries of livestock rubbing may very well have erased all trace.

NORTHERN APPROACHES

Whitecombe Moss

Hentoe Hill

Great Grassoms

Stoneside Hill

Crookley Beck

Bootle Fell

BOOTLE

MILLOM A595

WABERTHWAITE A595

Black Combe from Bootle main street

ASCENT
from Bootle

12 Park in the village off the main street opposite the church; alternatively, and with due sensitivity, on Fellgreen, above Fell Gate Cottage GR116885. The road running up from the village is a pleasure to tread. Notice the neat Cumbrian dyke walling at Under-wood Cottage. From Fellgreen the old Bootle Fell byway proceeds through a gate /hand-gate. Passing Nettle Crags, winding up then down through the Oldclose Gill dell, spot Gibson's Spout over to the right in Crookley Beck. The old road climbs to pass the top end of Cowcoppy, 'coppy' being a contraction for coppiced woodland; the present conifers are a poor substitute. Immediately beyond find a huge granite erratic block known as the Resting Stone. A fat finger-sized hole in the upper south side is hardly natural, presumably Bronze Age cup & ring symbolism. The open fell flanking the byway has contemporary field systems, but don't expect to be wowed.

As the open track bends left take the second green path rising right. This crosses over the bracken bank and slices through a cross-path, thus avoiding the broad sphagnum marsh. Descend into the Crookley Beck valley to ford the beck, passing over the hurdle gate, smartly followed by a concrete culvert ducting Grassgill Beck. Now heading southwest keep to the higher of the two subsequent green paths slanting across the fell-side, duly coming alongside the top of the enclosure wall. As a field-gate is spotted, just before the path begins to descend, take the obvious path left, up the gently rising ridge **2** – most commonly used as a descent route, so expect to meet someone. The author encountered two couples sitting in the heather midway up. They were taking a breather on their way down, and amid much laughter the girls said they were waiting for a bus!!

13 The Bootle Fell byway gives a grand insight into the style of roads before the advent of tarmac, for where opportune it is flanked with neat ditches to give run-off to minimise wash-out; this feature is known as a fosse. The Romans were adept at incorporating them on their engineered military roads, hence the Fosse Way, slicing diagonally across Britannia between Exeter to Lincoln, in effect the first Roman frontier of their island province. At a stile and gate the road becomes confined, pro-

Black Combe from Buckbarrow Beck

gressing onto the Corneyfell Road, heading on up to the road summit, beyond which the fell opens up once more. From this point it is practical to join the ridge wall over Stoneside Hill to the right. From the depression beyond this rock tor, the ridge fence onto Whitecombe Moss (see the Buckbarrow ridge route description) the ridge to Buckbarrow left is the more enticing. A circular walk can be created by traversing Buckbarrow and Whitfell, then crossing Burn Moor to follow the bridle-way down over the Corneyfell Road into the Kinmont Beck valley and by Kinmont Wood to the minor road leading back into Bootle.

The Summit

Retiring and something of an enigma, the gently domed top ensures that even from afar it is barely perceived, only hoving into view at the very last moment during any ascent. Seen from the south, notably Kirksanton, the portly south cairn pricks the skyline as the sham summit, the convex slope hiding the true top. Coming upon the shallow domed table-top, with the wind whistling off the ocean, the crude wind shelter has a greater than usual value. One may postulate who gathered the stones and over what period, though you'll be more grateful than quizzical. The OS column gains permanent benefit from this humble huddle of boulders. The majority of such pillars are now rendered redundant but this spot still serves cartographers, being a strategic point in the network of the global positioning system.

The south cairn, beyond the tarn in the intermediate dip, is not to be outdone, playing into the informal games of GPS users, as an unofficial GPS geocache station – the treasure discreetly stashed under a slate. The activity is to be respected, so don't go stealing anything, you're on your honour! William Wordsworth described the view from Black Combe: 'the amplest range of unobstructed prospect may be seen that British ground commands'. Well with so much ocean is there any wonder? The real view to adore lies within the northeasterly arc, with Scafell, Scafell Pike, Skiddaw and Helvellyn in view, Lakeland telescoped into a narrow mass a long arm's length away. In his collected poems *Sea to the West* that great Cumbrian observer Norman Nicholson saw from his Millom study window the fell's propensity to gather its own cap of cloud. 'Black Combe alone still hides', and 'beneath the Herdwick-fleece of mist you can feel the heave of the hill'. Having a climate all its own can be disadvantageous for the hapless fellwalker committed to an ascent when all else in Lakeland is clear.

The summit goal, on a football-pitch plateau, with a grandstand view to a crowd of fells

Safe Descents

The immediate concern is the broken precipice of Blackcombe Screes which lurks unseen close under the eastern lip of the summit plateau. As the majority of visitors will have come by the Whicham path, their minds will naturally turn to a straightforward retreat, though many wisely make a circuit upon the continuing bridle-path down the broad north ridge, cutting back south to Whitbeck (and Seaness for Whicham Church). Those that have come up the Whitecombe Beck valley may be lured into descending either side of Blackcombe Screes. In mist beware of the fall of the ground.

Ridge Route to...

BUCKBARROW   DESCENT 955*ft*   ASCENT 764*ft*   4.3miles

Follow the emerging path leading NE, watchful to keep a safe distance from profound declivity overlooking the deeply entrenched Whitecombe Beck valley. As the ground levels a narrow peaty trod draws close to a wire fence traversing Whitecombe Moss (tension causing it to emit a high-pitched hum during strong wind). As a barbed fence intervenes step over the plain fence, and keep to the west side of the continuing fence, thus avoiding the even wetter ground on Swinside Fell indicated by the rushes. The semblance of a path descends to cross a tall fence at the fence junction. Head straight on, keeping just left of the dwarf conifer shrubbery coming up to the netting fence beside the rising wall. Ideally a stile needs inserting adjacent to the Charity Chair sheepfold. Climb to the stony top of Stoneside Hill, a really good viewpoint for Buckbarrow. Descend, keeping the wall left, advancing to the summit of the Corneyfell Road (car parking space). Cross directly over, and keeping the wall close left, clamber over Great Paddy Crag before slanting half-right, weaving through boulders and outcropping to reach the summit cairn.

Head of the Whitecombe Beck valley

PANORAMA

Caw Fell | Pillar | Great Gable | Ill Crag | Crinkle Crags | Dollywaggon Pike | | Coniston Old Man | Harter Fell | | | Top o'Selside | | | Gummer's How

Haycock | Kirk Fell | Scafell Pike | | (Long Top) | Nethermost Pike | Grey Friar | | High Street | Tarn Crag | | | | | | | Burney

Robinson | Skiddaw | Esk Pike | Helvellyn | Great Carrs | Swirl How | Ill Bell | Kentmere Pike | | | Howgill Fells | | Blawith Knott

Scafell | Bowfell | Dow Crag | Caw | Grey Crag | | Barbon Fells

Burn Moor | Buckbarrow | Whitfell | Harter Fell | Stickle Pike

Hesk Fell | Green Crag

Be wary - this edge leads to the brink of Blackcombe Screes, from which the fell is named, treacherous ground in mist. There is no way down between the arrows

E

N

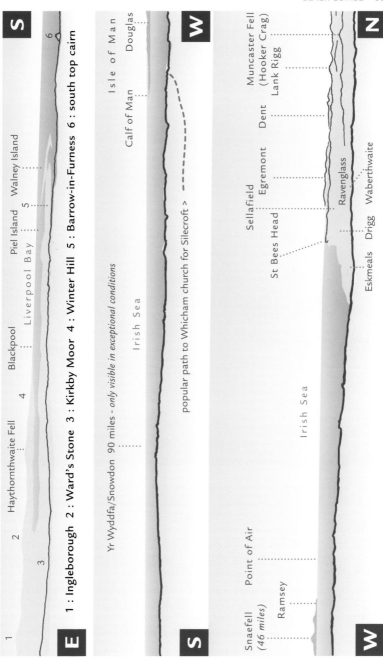

S

6

Haythornthwaite Fell
2
3

Blackpool
Piel Island   Walney Island
Liverpool Bay
5
4

1 : Ingleborough   2 : Ward's Stone   3 : Kirkby Moor   4 : Winter Hill   5 : Barrow-in-Furness   6 : south top cairn

E

W

Isle of Man   Douglas
Calf of Man

Yr Wyddfa/Snowdon 90 miles - *only visible in exceptional conditions*

Irish Sea

popular path to Whicham church for Silecroft >

S

Snaefell
(*46 miles*)
Ramsey
Point of Air

Irish Sea

W

N

Muncaster Fell
(Hooker Crag)
Lank Rigg

Sellafield
Egremont   Dent

St Bees Head

Ravenglass
Drigg   Waberthwaite
Eskmeals

W

BLACK FELL 2

Lying within the triangle of Skelwith Bridge, Hawkshead and Coniston, Black Fell forms the northerly backdrop summit on a comparatively low, intrinsically wild, undulating ridge focusing on Tarn Hows, that embodiment of human intervention to create a picturesque concept for public enjoyment. Tarn Hows magical mix of trees, rock and water was the brainchild of James Marshall, a wealthy linen magnate and Leeds MP, who moved to Monk Coniston in the 1860s.

This landscaping was both inspired and problematic for Marshall. He stocked the tarns with trout, only to have them consumed by pike. Frustrated, he drained the tarns, re-filling them after two years, but the damp ground harboured pike eggs and the voracious aquatic monster

322 *metres*   1,056 *feet*

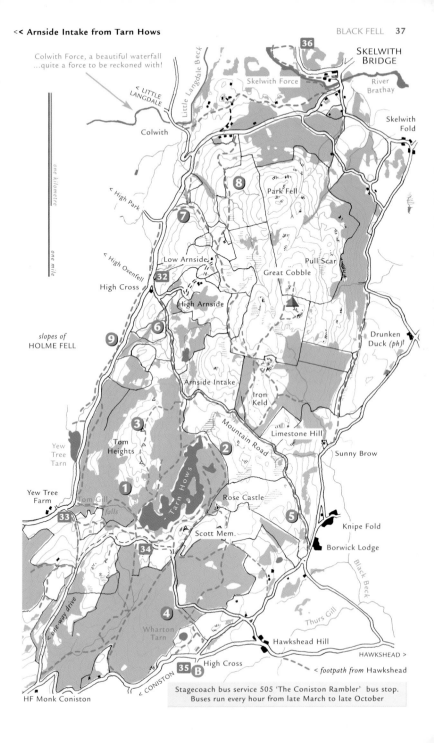

Colwith Force, a beautiful waterfall
...quite a force to be reckoned with!

SKELWITH
BRIDGE

36

Skelwith Force

River
Brathay

< LITTLE
LANGDALE

Little Langdale Beck

Skelwith
Fold

Colwith

8

Park Fell

7

Pull Scar

< High Park

Low Arnside

Great Cobble

32

High Cross

High Arnside

Drunken
Duck *(ph)*

6

9

slopes of
HOLME FELL

Arnside Intake

Iron
Keld

3

Tom
Heights

Mountain Road

Limestone Hill

2

Sunny Brow

Yew
Tree
Tarn

1

Tarn Hows

Yew Tree
Farm

Tom Gill

Rose Castle

falls

5

Knipe Fold

33

Borwick Lodge

Scott Mem.

34

Black Beck

one kilometre

one mile

4

Thurs Gill

Wharton
Tarn

one-way drive

Hawkshead Hill

HAWKSHEAD >

35 B

High Cross

< *footpath from Hawkshead*

< CONISTON

HF Monk Coniston

Stagecoach bus service 505 'The Coniston Rambler' bus stop.
Buses run every hour from late March to late October

Wetherlam
from Tarn Hows

took any new stock. In 1920 a new dam was constructed just above Yew Tree Farm; the snag this time – it was built on a geological fault. Every twenty years or so a certain re-engineering of a leaking dam is therefore necessary. In the time of the Marshall family, there was but a linear path running along the east side of Tarn Hows to Rose Castle, a folly doubling as a quarryman's abode.

Today the whole wonderful setting can be delightfully enjoyed by all. The National Trust are set on a programme of care, seeking to re-create an appropriately scenic whole. Sir Samuel Scott of Windermere acquired Tarn Hows for the Trust when he bought the whole estate from Mrs Beatrix Heelis (better known as Beatrix Potter). She had acquired it in 1930 when the Marshalls had to sell to recoup family losses after the First World War. Scott's generosity and far-sightedness is marked by a plaque set on the head-land east of the tarns beyond the disabled car park. Anyone who wanders from off the Hawkshead/Coniston road will be overwhelmed by the stately majesty of this arboretum nurtured by the Marshalls and beautifully sustained by the Trust.

Evidently the fell-name derived from the eastern perspective, from where afternoon and evening light casts shadows down its steep slopes: patrons tumbling out of the fashionable eating and drinking house, the Drunken Duck Inn, will detect its vague dark outline too!

View over Tarn Hows to Black Fell from the Scott memorial

Walkers happily intent on the Cumbria Way, heading north from Coniston, understandably relish their encounter with Tarn Hows, but the majority are unaware of Black Crag. Cross-country routes have that knack of missing isolated lime-lit locations when they fit awkwardly with the through-route grand design. The wear on the one path to the top shows that the actual number of visitors is quite modest, restricted to a small discerning proportion of the multitude who stroll in the environs of Tarn Hows. The summit is the perfect place to come for a first inspection of this marvellous landscape, the lie of the high land and the low land superbly displayed.

ASCENT *from Tarn Hows*

1 Visitors are naturally drawn to park at the main Tarn Hows car park. However, the far more exciting walk launches from the smaller car park at Tom Gill. A stepped path climbs in harmony with the north bank of the beck in woodland, particularly revelling in the graceful waterfall in the upper section, below the dam. Of the two paths climbing on the south side, directly from the car park, one in the stony lane joins the one-way road, the other, branches left, winding up pasture. Both have their special merit for easy descents. **2** From the dam a broad path, fit for an urban park, proceeds north. Every Tom, Dick and Harry, whether with dog accomplice or not, comes this way, the majority simply enacting a clockwise circumnavigation of the tarn, admiring the rocky, marshy wild periphery as from a cage. The northern continuation leads on to meet the fell-crossing lane known as the Mountain Road, where Black Fell proper begins. **3** Readers of this guide will need no second invitation to venture onto the wonderfully undulating top of Tom Heights. As the path makes the first rise into woodland, go sharp left under an ageing larch. An obvious path climbing the bank winds up onto the rising ridge, gaily decked with birch. Each stepped knoll is marked with a cairn. The summit cairn is a definite place to pause perhaps wondering where all

Windermere cairn

The Mountain Road

the people have gone. Gaze westward over Holme Fell to Wetherlam and north-eastward to Black Fell, backed by the Near Eastern Fells. It seems no height has been climbed, but the fell wildness is profound. The ridge path threads on down through the tough growth. Taking damp ground in your stride, pass another prominent cairn to reach the broad path from the Tarns at the ladder-stile/gate entry into the Mountain Road. Follow this lane right (east), bound for the Iron Keld enclosure with two access points. **4** Walkers occasionally approach Tarn Hows from Hawkshead village, a footpath coming up to meet the road at Hawkshead Hill. Bus travellers and motorists can better start at High Cross, at the northern tip of Grisedale Forest, following a path by Wharton Tarn to join the route beside the Tarns. **5** Alternatively, follow the minor road to Knipe Fold, entering the Mountain Road at Borwick Lodge. Ascend the lane taking the first kissing-gate entry into the Iron Keld enclosure, keep to

Low Arnside from the summit, backed by the fells at the head of the Langdales

the track then path which sweeps up northwestward to meet the main track at the kissing-gate at the top of the enclosure. **6** From Oxenfell High Cross the Mountain Road begins as a proper road, being access for High Arnside Farm, but quickly turns into a gravel trackway. It is a lovely walk with a succession of scenic turns. Passing the Tarns access gate, the lane winds up and levels under Arnside Intake, advancing to a gate entry, left, into Iron Keld (definition: 'iron well'). The National Trust has made considerable strides in removing most of the misfit conifer trees in the enclosure, seeking to restore a more natural wooded habitat within the overall context of the estate. They certainly take their custodianship of this national treasure seriously.

North to Helvellyn and Fairfield from Great Cobble

ASCENT *from Oxen Fell and Skelwith Bridge*

7 An excellent 'quick way to the top' embarks from the High Park road-end upon a footpath commencing from a gate and short wooded lane, leading east. This descends briefly with a wall left, then, where another footpath joins at a gate, climbs the pasture beside the same wall to a gate, coming up to merge with the Park Fell bridleway; keep right to pass Low Arnside. **8** From Skelwith Bridge and the Brathay vale the National Trust Silverthwaite car park is the best starting point. This gives access to the riverbank path heading serenely downstream. Entering woodland, tight by the busy road, the river becomes tumultuous. Skelwith Force is a real force to be reckoned with and admired. The fuming falls can be viewed from both banks. The footpath passes on by the Kirkstone Quarry workshops to cross Skelwith Bridge. Keeping company with the Cumbria Way, head west via Park Farm to Low Colwith. Go left, up the road, turning right with the A 593; branch right after a bus shelter via a gate onto the bridleway climbing the northwestern side of Park Fell. The open track winds up with excellent views back to Lingmoor Fell and the great swelling heights about Great Langdale. By gates the track passes a sheep-wash fold *(right)*, winds on by the outlying Low Arnside, a charming holiday cottage steading connected

with High Arnside Farm. Coming up to the top of the Iron Keld enclosure, find the path to the summit branching left. **9** This is of value to walkers wishing to complete an off-road circuit of the fell, having begun at Tom Gill. A footpath can be followed, coming off route **7**; it rises, fenced, inside the pasture beside the road from the High Park road-end, continuing directly over at Oxen Fell High Cross, dipping down into the wooded dell beneath Holme Fell. Either cross the road at a ladder-stile before Yew Tree Tarn to trace the woodland path under Tom Heights, or follow the path on the western side of the tarn.

The Summit

A conclusive rock summit is adorned with a stone-built OS pillar. Old maps give it the somewhat over-egged name Black Crag. While it is generally true that it is better to travel than to arrive, here is a spot well worth arriving at. Black Fell has its aficionados, regulars who readily extol its virtues as a place to soak up a rejuvenating view, time and again. In the course of the preparation of this guide the author made just two visits, each time meeting regulars whose love of the landscape was

reinvigorated by this one place. The view is an utter joy, the Coniston Fells loom large to the west, with the fells simply crowding into the great northerly arc, Scafell Pike and Great End making sneaky guest appearances either side of Bowfell. Also in view are the Langdale Pikes and Blencathra through the Thirlmere trench, with Helvellyn and Fairfield, Red Screes and the Kentmere Fells leading to a long Pennine skyline beyond Windermere. Arguably the best views in that direction are to found on the ridge over the ladder-stile, purposefully installed to facilitate visitors' desire to venture onto the Great Cobble headland. There is no means of reaching a public road from this northerly enclosure, and for all the presence of cairns on the lower north top of Park Fell, walkers are encouraged to step back over the ladder-stile and retreat the way they arrived. Well, not quite, because there is a prominent viewpoint cairn down on the eastern shoulder of the fell, some 200 metres away, definitely a place to frequent and enjoy the wooded vale towards Windermere. Though flagging from age, its retains much of its evidently original fine construction. So at busy times walkers have at least three excellent viewing stations that in their moments they can call their own.

Safe Descents

Hardly applicable other than to advise walkers not to clamber over walls or stray from paths as route matters are set in stone, so to speak, and woodland thicket and giraffe-high bracken await the wayward wanderer. Simply backtrack to Iron Keld, then either take the bridle-path by Low Arnside, or pass on down through the newly opened forestry to join the Mountain Road for points east, west or south.

Black Fell from Holme Fell

PANORAMA

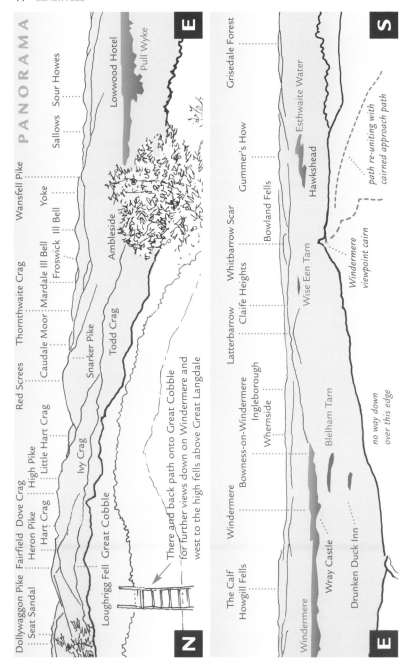

E

Pull Wyke
Lowwood Hotel
Sour Howes
Sallows
Wansfell Pike
Yoke
Ill Bell
Froswick
Mardale Ill Bell
Thornthwaite Crag
Caudale Moor
Red Screes
Little Hart Crag
High Pike
Fairfield   Dove Crag
Hart Crag
Heron Pike
Dollywaggon Pike
Seat Sandal

Ambleside
Snarker Pike
Todd Crag
Ivy Crag
Loughrigg Fell   Great Cobble

N

There and back path onto Great Cobble for further views down on Windermere and west to the high fells above Great Langdale

---

S

Grisedale Forest
Esthwaite Water
Gummer's How
Hawkshead
Whitbarrow Scar
Bowland Fells
Latterbarrow
Claife Heights
Wise Een Tarn
Bowness-on-Windermere
Ingleborough
Whernside
Windermere
Blelham Tarn
The Calf
Howgill Fells
Wray Castle
Drunken Duck Inn
Windermere

Windermere viewpoint cairn

path re-uniting with cairned approach path

no way down over this edge

E

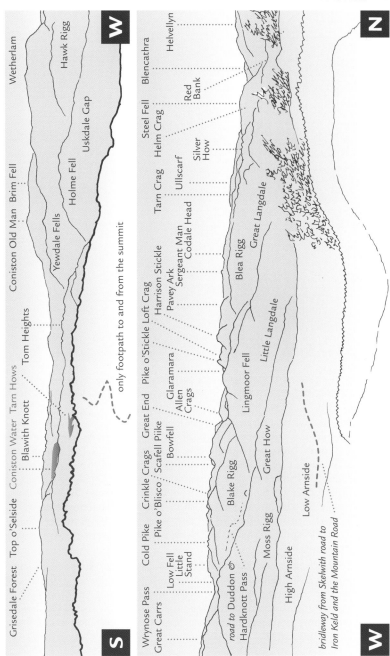

S panel (top):

Griesdale Forest · Top o'Selside · Coniston Water · Tarn Hows · Tom Heights · Coniston Old Man · Brim Fell · Wetherlam

Blawith Knott · Yewdale Fells · Holme Fell · Uskdale Gap · Hawk Rigg

only footpath to and from the summit

W / N / W panel (bottom):

Wrynose Pass · Great Carrs · Cold Pike · Crinkle Crags · Pike o'Blisco · Scafell Pike · Great End · Pike o'Stickle · Loft Crag · Harrison Stickle · Pavey Ark · Sergeant Man · Codale Head · Tarn Crag · Ullscarf · Silver How · Steel Fell · Helm Crag · Red Bank · Blencathra · Helvellyn

Low Fell · Little Stand · Bowfell · Glaramara · Allen Crags · Lingmoor Fell · Great Langdale · Blea Rigg

Blake Rigg · Little Langdale

road to Duddon & Hardknott Pass

Moss Rigg · Great How

High Arnside · Low Arnside

bridleway from Skelwith road to Iron Keld and the Mountain Road

BRIM FELL

Literally the skyline 'brim' of the Coppermines valley, composing the lion's share of the Old Man ridge, and yet inevitably subjugated to ancillary rank, and cradling two wind-whipped tarns, Levers and Low Water, either side of a blunt ridge which ends abruptly upon Raven Tor. Below the cliff runs the lateral Boulder valley, which in its lower portion harbours some quite extraordinarily chunks of rock, of which the Pudding Stone is the biggest: a boulder problem with one easy scrambling ascent for those with the aptitude and inclination. At the head of the Boulder valley lie fenced clefts associated with possibly the oldest copper mine in the area, Paddy End. The most striking feature is Simon's Nick, prominent during the ascent of Leverswater Beck, beneath which spill extensive areas of the characteristic brown iron oxide spoil scree.

With so much attention directed at the Old Man one suspects anyone seen climbing Brim Fell is there by mistake! Well, let's be charitable, I have twice encountered walkers on the upper slopes of Brim Fell in glorious sunshine nervously enquiring 'was this the way to the Old Man'. It appears some walkers reach Low Water veer over to its outflow, thinking they are on the main path, and then having crossed the out-

795 *metres*   2,608 *feet*

Do not attempt to
follow the path
marked on OS maps
apparently descending
due west from Levers
Hause; there isn't one
and the scree is
unforgiving!

SWIRL HOW
804m 2,638ft

Calf Cove

The Prison   old
                    copper mine

Great How Crags

slopes of
GREY FRIAR

Little How Crags   slopes of
                                    WETHERLAM

Seathwaite   old
Tarn   copper mines   Levers Hause

                                    Levers
                                    Water   Paddy End
                                                 Copper Mine

Wray Crags   Cove   Simon's Nick
                                                old copper
                            Raven Tor   mine

                                        Boulder Valley

                                    The Pudding
                                    Stone
Goat's Hause   active
                                            slate quarry

                            Low
                            Water
                                old slate
                                quarries

DOW CRAG
778m 2,553ft

                    CONISTON OLD MAN
                    803m 2,635ft
Goat's
Water

flow, find any hint of a path disap-
pears. Instead of backtracking they
head on up the inviting grassy slope
to the saddle to the rear of Raven Tor
and mount Brim Fell, oblivious of
their error. What they consider a hor-
ror in fact is a master-stroke, for this
is the sweetest way onto the main
ridge, believe me. Viewed from the
west, Brim Fell has few endearing

Leverswater Dam and Raven Tor

qualities, its shattered cliff and scree a conclusive eastern headwall of
the Seathwaite Tarn valley. So the unrealistic marking of a footpath into
this wild hollow from Levers Hause is a cruel mystery that Ordnance
Survey mapping should rectify for the sake of delicate ankles and necks.
One suspects many walkers have relied on their otherwise meticulous
cartography in hostile conditions, and erroneously presumed this a safe
recourse. It isn't!

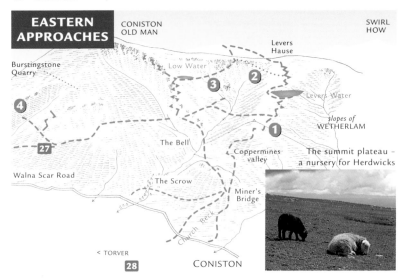

EASTERN APPROACHES

CONISTON OLD MAN

SWIRL HOW

Levers Hause

Burstingstone Quarry

Low Water

Levers Water

slopes of WETHERLAM

The Bell

Coppermines valley

The summit plateau – a nursery for Herdwicks

Walna Scar Road

The Scrow

Miner's Bridge

Church Beck

< TORVER

CONISTON

ASCENT *from the Coppermines valley*

Brimful of energy? So to walk. **1** Starting from the focal bridge beside the Black Bull Hotel and brewery in Coniston main street, follow either the road and open valley access track on the north side of Church Beck, or begin, along the Walna Scar Road, turning right after the Sun Hotel, signposted to the 'Old Man' via Dixon's Ground. Approaching Miner's Bridge cross over, and join the main valley track leading on by the Coppermines Youth Hostel, the former copper mine captain's office. The continuing track winds up to end at the outflow and dam of Levers Water; cradled in a wild corrie rimmed with crags, the large boulder in the tarn close by is often the perch of herring gulls. The upper stage of the ascent is dominated by the massive cleft of Simon's Nick, part of the Paddy End copper workings. Go left along the low dam skirting the tarn, rising to pass under the fenced mine workings at the rear of Simon's Nick. Be warned: the dark holes thus corralled are a death trap, shafts run many hundreds of feet down into the fell, tracing the rich veins of copper sulphite – the preserve of well-equipped speleologists. Follow the clear, if rough, path contouring above the tarn beneath Raven Tor; fording a gill the path veers uphill with Cove Gill, steeper sections suitably pitched. Little How Crags feature up to the right. Watch to keep to the well-made path, avoiding the loose scree which appears to be the direct way. The ground steepens still further with consistent pitching zig-zagging to Levers Hause, where the main ridge route is joined. Turn left, due south to reach the summit cairn. **2** An intriguing alternative branches south before the main stepped section begins, accompanies Cove Gill into the Cove recess, slipping over a saddle to find a faint path across a loose section leading to the skyline col directly behind Raven Tor. All on easy ground, nonetheless, in mist I suggest you stay with the path to Levers Hause.

3 The way up from Low Water is a splendid route, predominantly on grass, something one cannot say about the quarryman's path onto the Old Man. Follow the walkers' highway, described in the Coniston Old Man chapter (route **1**). Branch right upon arrival at Low Water, threading through the large boulders haphazardly gathered among the moraine. Cross the outflow. Head north up the grassy slope to the saddle to the rear of Raven Tor. Make a point of visiting the cairned top of the Tor, up the bank right, and look through the notch across the airy gulf to Great How Crags. From the saddle turn left (due west) where minor broken outcropping leads onto the plateau. Pass a large cairn amongst clitter en route to the main summit cairn.

Mine enthusiast abseiling into the Simon's Nick/Paddy End copper mine, adjacent to Levers Water

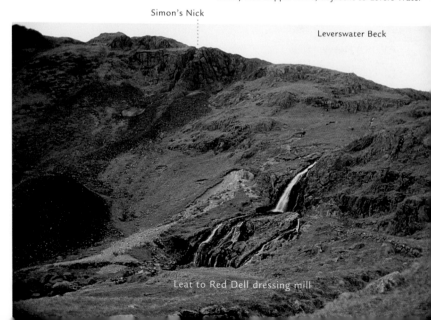

Simon's Nick

Leverswater Beck

Leat to Red Dell dressing mill

ASCENT *from Walna Scar Road*

4 By normal convention this route, via Goat's Hause, is used as an easy-on-the-knees descent, ideal for the round trip. Refer to Coniston Old Man route **1**. On the regular path curving up from Goat's Hause branch half-left, at will, climbing the grass slope direct to the summit.

The Summit

For all the fell-top is gently domed and almost bereft of surface features, the summit cairn, composed of thick wafers of bedrock slate, is a gem, a solid pile, far grander than the cairn on Swirl How. The view is only hampered by the extent of the plateau but it is brimful of detail as the panorama shows.

Safe Descents

In misty conditions put your faith in either Levers Hause, due N, with its well-pitched path E leading down to Levers Water, or Goat's Hause SW, with a steady descent S down by Goat's Water and the Cove to join the Walna Scar Road, in both instances seeking the shelter of Coniston. Goat's Hause also provides a safe line NW into the Seathwaite Tarn valley for the Duddon.

Ridge Routes to...

CONISTON OLD MAN   DESCENT 80*ft*   ASCENT 108*ft*   0.5 miles

Head S, keeping steep ground several strides-length to the left.

DOW CRAG   DESCENT 490*ft*   ASCENT 425*ft*   0.8 miles

Descend the grassy slope SW to Goat's Hause, joining the regular path curving round from W to S to the summit bastion.

SWIRL HOW   DESCENT 370*ft*   ASCENT 400*ft*   1.5 miles

Follow the ridge on its steady descent to Levers Hause, which like Link Hause on the Fairfield Horseshoe is not a cross-over pass! A definite path contours above Calf Cove towards the namesake Fairfield saddle beneath Grey Friar, while the actual ridge route climbs NNE, glancing by the consecutive tops of Little, then the more significant peak of Great How Crags. Beyond, weave through the irregular surface outcropping to the summit.

Two views from the north ridge to *(above)* Seathwaite Tarn and *(below)* Swirl How

PANORAMA

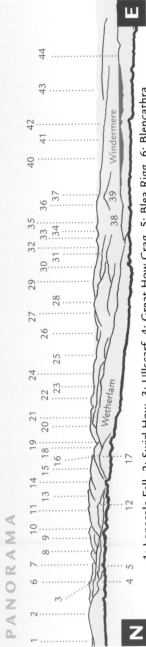

N · E

1: Lonscale Fell 2: Swirl How 3: Ullscarf 4: Great How Crag 5: Blea Rigg 6: Blencathra
7: Bannerdale Crags 8: Clough Head 9: Watson's Dodd 10: Great Dodd 11: Helvellyn Little Man 12: Steel Fell
13: Helvellyn 14: Nethermost Pike 15: Dollywaggon Pike 16: Seat Sandal 17: Black Sails 18: Little Mell Fell
19: Grisedale Hause 20: Fairfield 21: Great Rigg 22: Hart Crag 23: Heron Pike 24: Dove Crag 25: High Pike
26: Rest Dodd 27: Rampsgill Head 28: Red Screes 29: High Street 30: Thornthwaite Crag 31: Troutbeck Tongue
32: Mardale Ill Bell 33: Froswick 34: Harter Fell 35: Ill Bell 36: Yoke 37: Kentmere Pike 38: Black Fell
39: Wansfell Pike 40: Sallows 41: Sour Howes 42: Shap Fells 43: Stainmore Forest 44: Latterbarrow

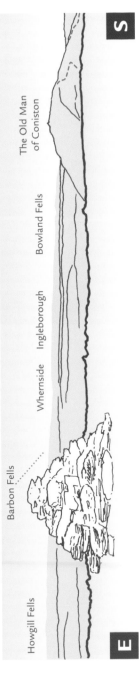

S · E

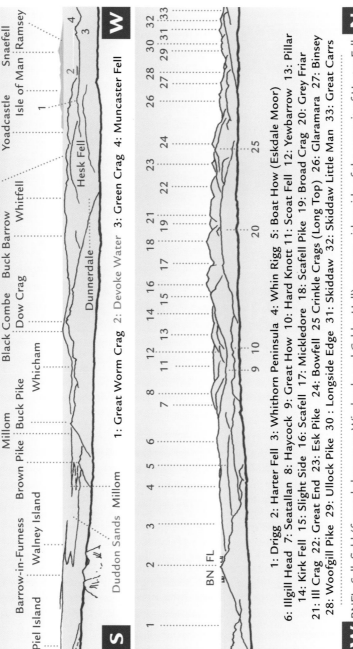

S

Piel Island
Barrow-in-Furness   Walney Island
Brown Pike
Millom
Buck Pike
Black Combe   Buck Barrow
Whicham
Dow Crag
Whitfell
Stainton Pike
Yoadcastle
Snaefell
Isle of Man Ramsey

Duddon Sands Millom

Dunnerdale

Hesk Fell

W

1: Great Worm Crag 2: Devoke Water 3: Green Crag 4: Muncaster Fell

N

BN FL

W

1: Drigg 2: Harter Fell 3: Whithorn Peninsula 4: Whin Rigg 5: Boat How (Eskdale Moor)
6: Illgill Head 7: Seatallan 8: Haycock 9: Great How 10: Hard Knott 11: Scoat Fell 12: Yewbarrow 13: Pillar
14: Kirk Fell 15: Slight Side 16: Scafell 17: Mickledore 18: Scafell Pike 19: Broad Crag 20: Grey Friar
21: Ill Crag 22: Great End 23: Esk Pike 24: Bowfell 25 Crinkle Crags (Long Top) 26: Glaramara 27: Binsey
28: Woofgill Pike 29: Ullock Pike 30 : Longside Edge 31: Skiddaw 32: Skiddaw Little Man 33: Great Carrs

BNFL: Sellafield (formerly known as Windscale and Calder Hall) appears either side of the summit of Harter Fell

BUCKBARROW 4

Definition: 'the gathering place of young bucks' (red deer): older bucks (Homo sapiens) now have the run of the place – the deer have fled. The summit area is an oasis of mountain Lakeland, with three, if not four rocky tops to explore. It shares with the crest of Stoneside Hill a sense of rugged wildness, a welcome contrast to the sleeker lines of Black Combe and Whitfell. Access to this fell top just could not be easier, a gently rising ridge wall leads from the Corneyfell Road summit, arrowing into the midriff of the summit mass on Great Paddy Crag, though the actual summit is well defended with rocky ground.

Fellwalkers eyeing linear outings will see the pleasure in a 'Bootle to Boot' connection, or the 'Black Combe to Devoke Water' ridge route. In either case Buckbarrow makes a most satisfying early objective. The uninviting fenced western slopes of Prior Park rise from the Corneyfell Road, the name indicative of medieval monastic deer enclosure. Eastern slopes run down over the unlikely tilled Plough Fell, angling south over Thwaites Fell to end in the old coppice woodland at the foot of the Duddon valley. Here is possibly the fell's greatest treasure, namely the remarkably extant remains of Duddon Bridge iron blast furnace which ran on locally sourced charcoal, succumbing to the greater efficiency of coke in 1867. A bridleway from the site climbs onto the fell, via Barrow.

549 *metres*   1,801 *feet*

ASCENT *from Corney Fell*

1 Park at the road summit, follow the clear path north in harmony with the ridge wall. As Great Paddy Crag rears there is the element of choice. Either slant up right threading up via boulders and outcropping onto the summit – spasmodic hints of a path. Or, bear left, keeping beside the fence under the boulder bank, passing a curious wind-shelter-like assemblage. Head WNW to a gateway, mount the easy slope to reach the western scarp-top summit of Kinmont Buckbarrow. The cairn, resting upon an ancient cairn, is a down-sized version of the Whitfell summit, though this top surveys a great sweep of land and ocean. One may backtrack to the gateway and slant half-left via a broken wall to reach the main summit up the boulder slope, or continue with the ridge path down as for Littlecell Bottom and Whitfell. **2** The honest ascent starts from Bootle, following the old road up from Fellgreen. A pleasure to stride, the open byway is a firm green ribbon winding up into a lane to meet the Corneyfell Road some 230 metres west of the road summit.

ASCENT *from Buckbarrow Bridge*

3 Follow the green track direct from the open road, originally made for peat extraction on the plateau of Burn Moor. Watch for the shepherd's quad wheel-marks forking right off the green-way short of Hare Raise – if you meet the said quad in misty conditions then it may be hair-raising! Contour round the northern side of the Littlecell Bottom marsh linking up with the ridge path coming off Burn Moor. Head south, perhaps keeping among the outcropping for greater interest up to the summit.

The Summit

This rocky crest would not be out of place anywhere in Lakeland, in fact it is very reminiscent of Cold Pike. The view is very different, though deserves to be savoured, with Whitfell drawing attention north to the majesty of the central Lakes.

The summit from Kinmont Buckbarrow

Safe Descents

Simple, follow the ridge wall S off Great Paddy Crag ('frog's rocks') to the summit of the Corneyfell Road. The regularity of the traffic may entice you to thumb a lift! The nearest comfort is Bootle, down the Old Fell Road which branches initially as a lane, WSW some 180 metres W of the road summit.

Ridge Routes to...

BLACK COMBE   DESCENT 764ft   ASCENT 955ft   4.3 miles

For much of the way a wall, then a fence, act as guides; though legitimately with Open Access, presently there are no stiles. Follow the ridge wall off Great Paddy Crag, crossing the Corneyfell Road, mounting onto the rocky hillock of Stoneside Hill. Descend S seeking a suitable gap through the decrepit wall and compensatory netting fence near the sheepfold at Charity Chair. Pass the stunted conifer spinney, skip over
continued on facing page >>

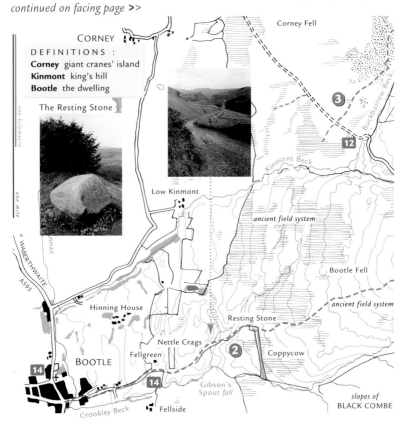

CORNEY

DEFINITIONS :
Corney giant cranes' island
Kinmont king's hill
Bootle the dwelling

The Resting Stone

Corney Fell

Low Kinmont

ancient field system

Bootle Fell

ancient field system

Hinning House

Nettle Crags

Fellgreen

Resting Stone

Coppycow

BOOTLE

Gibson's
Spout *fall*

Crookley Beck   Fellside

slopes of
BLACK COMBE

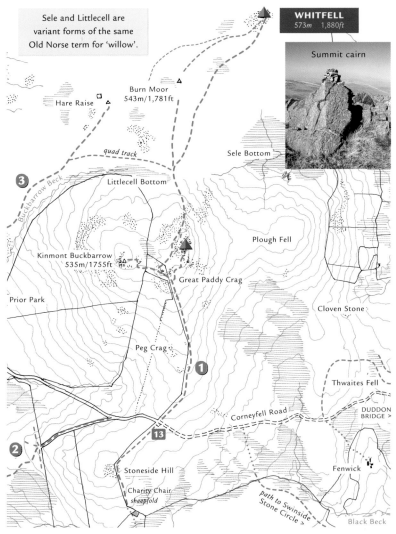

Sele and Littlecell are variant forms of the same Old Norse term for 'willow'.

WHITFELL
573m 1,880ft

Summit cairn

Burn Moor
543m/1,781ft

Hare Raise

quad track

Sele Bottom

3

Buckbarrow Beck

Littlecell Bottom

Plough Fell

Kinmont Buckbarrow
535m/1755ft

Great Paddy Crag

Prior Park

Cloven Stone

Peg Crag

1

Thwaites Fell

DUDDON
BRIDGE >

Corneyfell Road

13

2

Stoneside Hill

Fenwick

Charity Chair
sheepfold

path to Swinside
Stone Circle >

Black Beck

the ditch, tracing a low bank to a fence junction. Step over this tall obstacle, continuing up the rough moorland with the fence to the left. Nearing the brow, step over the plain fence immediately beyond the barbed fence junction and continue over Whitecombe Moss, to join with the path climbing out of the Whitecombe Beck valley, running above the steep escarpment of Whitecombe Screes and rise onto the summit SW.

WHITFELL   DESCENT 236ft ASCENT 315ft   1.4 miles

Head N, via Littlecell Bottom, drawing across Burn Moor's E slopes.

PANORAMA

N

Haycock Pillar
Scoat Fell : 1 Kirk Fell   2   3   4   5   6   7   Bowfell 10 11   12   13 Grey Friar 14   15 Dow Crag 16 17 White Pike Caw Stickle Pike
                                                                9   Great Stickle
Red Pike Illgill Head
Burn Moor
Whitfell

The Pike

Plough Fell

1: Yewbarrow 2: Robinson 3: Great Gable 4: Scafell
5: Scafell Pike 6: Ill Crag 7: Esk Pike 8: Hesk Fell
9: Green Crag 10: Crinkle Crags (Long Top)
11: Harter Fell 12: Cold Pike 13: Helvellyn
14: Swirl How 15: Brim Fell
16: Coniston Old Man 17: Walna Scar

E

S

Swinside Fell

Barrow-in-Furness

Askam-in-Furness

The Knott

Kirkby Moor

Foxfield

Bowland Fells

Barrow

Broughton-in-Furness

Ingleborough

Dunnerdale

Duddon Estuary

E

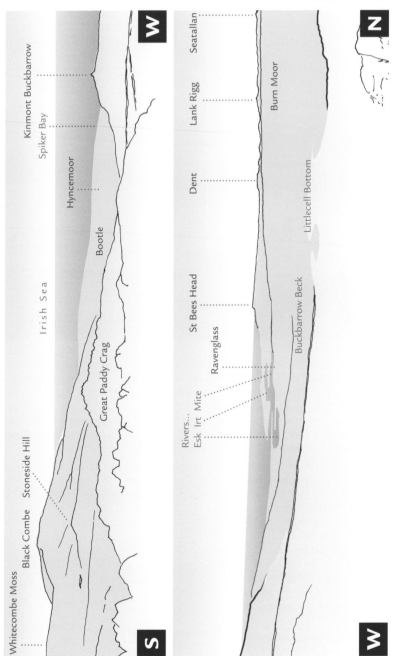

W

Whitecombe Moss

Black Combe   Stoneside Hill

Irish Sea

Great Paddy Crag

Bootle

Hyncemoor

Spiker Bay

Kinmont Buckbarrow

S

N

W

Seatallan

Lank Rigg

Dent

St Bees Head

Ravenglass

Rivers...
Esk Irt Mite

Burn Moor

Littlecell Bottom

Buckbarrow Beck

Viewed from Ulpha this is a real peak, a fell that simply demands to be climbed. Caw is highly individual and holds a disproportionate prominence, catching the eye from as far away as the M6. From within the Duddon its gracefully chiselled profile gives it a presence. Stand on its summit and know its central importance to an appreciation of that most beautiful of dales. The northern slopes falling quickly away beneath one's feet extend a fabulous outlook towards the Scafells.

The fell-name sounds corvine, though is probably associated with a former breeding ground of red deer. Defined east and west by the Lickle and Duddon, the former a strange river-name with no parallels; the earliest known spelling of c.1180 is 'Licul'. Bridle tracks strap both flanks, giving interesting approach options. There is much rock evident on all sides, its several subsidiary pikes adding immeasurably to any ascent.

Outlook from the mouth
of the Caw slate mine

529 *metres*   1,736 *feet*

slopes of
Wallowbarrow Heald
GREEN CRAG

SEATHWAITE

Moss Crag

River Duddon

46

Newfield Inn

tank

2

HALL
DUNNERDALE

1

Dobby Shaw

Dawson
Pike

Low Hall

Yaud Mire

*old slate
mine*

Green Pikes

Pikes

Park Head Road

Natty
Bridge

Tail Crag

Brock Barrow

3

Fox Haw

5

Kiln
Bank

6

4

7

Long Mire Beck

Stephenson Ground

23

*old slate
quarries*

The Knott

*road
gate*

Jackson Ground

Water Yeat Bridge

Hoses

25

STICKLE PIKE
375m 1,234ft

Raven's Crag

Stainton
Ground

Carter Ground

The Hawk

Ball Hall

TORVER >

The Knott

Bracelet Moor

< BROUGHTON-
IN-FURNESS

BROUGHTON
MILLS >

River Lickle

< BROUGHTON-
IN-FURNESS

Lind End

one kilometre   *one mile*

ASCENT *from Seathwaite*

1 From the road bend 90 metres east of the Newfield Inn, pass through the gated sheep pen onto the rough cart-track of Park Head Road up by a gate, close to Old Park Beck; seek the stone-retained incline branching up left *(see right)*. Stride at ease up the carpet-soft turf, in contrast to the grinding graft of the hobnailed slate quarrymen and their ponies for whom this steep way was a laborious trod. The tooling shed and spoil tip mark the end of the path. The mine level will invite a tentative peep. To judge by the quantity of slate in the tip the level must run deep into Caw's core. (Sorry, couldn't resist that one!) The hint

Caw slate mine incline

of a continuing path now mounts the grassy rake above (SW), rising to the summit. **2** A less than obvious drove-way branches off the Park Head Road straight on from the sheep pens. Keep Gobling Beck to the left in rising over marshy ground, then up a bracken bank, fording the beck left, to curve round a rushy patch, now onto a far more assured green path. This slips through a gateway (note the old stoup stone lying here) and contours NE before winding up the enclosure to a hurdle in the boundary wall. Either trend right to clamber over Green Pikes or keep with the continuing path up Yaud Mire to embark on the easier ridge heading SW to the summit of Pikes. Descend, via a ramp, into the hollow with more than the hint of a ridge path advancing to the main summit mass.

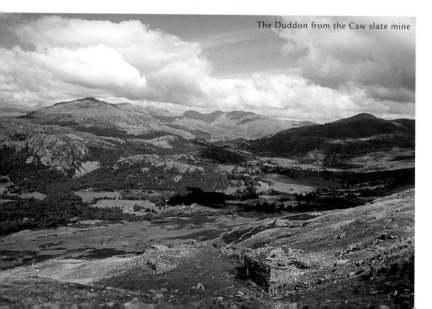

The Duddon from the Caw slate mine

ASCENT *from the Lickle valley*

Four routes stem from the vicinity of Water Yeat Bridge GR 239930, situated two miles upstream of Broughton Mills, at the edge of the Broughton Moor Forest Enterprise estate. **3** From the forest gate, 275 metres to the south of the bridge GR 239928, enter the part-cleared plantation beneath the Knott, on a clear if infrequently used forest track. Three wheeling buzzards above the tall conifer stand indignantly responded to the author's presence. The track wends up the valley, nearing the juvenile Lickle with the rough slopes of Caw clearly in view. On the far bank an old bridle-path, begin-

Mountain bikers on the road up to Stephenson Ground

ning at Stephenson Ground, is an excellent alternative upper valley route. As the mature plantation gives way to younger stock, spot a path branching down left; there is no compunction to follow apart from visiting the elegant flag footbridge otherwise hidden from the track. Should you be thus lured and be content to proceed on the west bank path, pass through a wall gate to merge with the continuation of the forest track on the open fell beyond Natty Bridge. Keeping to the forest track, pause at the next turning space to admire, left, the waterfall spilling from the combe south of Pikes. Soon the track ends at a stile short of an attractive ravine. A suitably spruce, if not dapper, wooden bridge has replaced an evidently sturdy stone-arched bridge, almost entirely washed away. A fragment remains, hinting at the lost delight of the old Natty Bridge. Cascades seen from the bridge give further cause to pause; the term 'natty' applied here means a 'chattering stream'. The path meets up with the path from the western bank and heads on up the damp fell towards a shallow pass, ultimate destination the old Walna Scar quarry and road. Note a path bearing sharply right with a small outcrop left, round the outcrop heading in a westerly direction, with no hint of a path. Clamber onto the top of the first rise, look northeastward to the dominant peak of White Pike, the terminating prow of Walna Scar and southern limit of the principal mountain mass of the Coniston group: most impressive.

With only the occasional faint hint of a path, walk on up the southwesterly trending ridge, passing a lovely pool en route to the rocky peak of Pikes, which is a good intermediate point to rest and consider the Duddon

Flag footbridge in the upper Lickle valley

Black Combe from Tail Crag

scene. A path trends down right from this top, into the hollow, before climbing to the main summit; again in mist the tracing path would be an uncertain guide. The path becomes slightly more conspicuous as it momentarily splits before the steep final pull to the pillar.

4 Another ascent from Water Yeat Bridge winds uphill close to farmhouse at Stephenson Ground. Take the gate right immediately short of the farmhouse, where two bridleways start, signed respectively 'Walna Scar' and 'Seathwaite'. Take the latter path, passing up by the house to enter a walled lane. The walling deserves a close look, particularly after the ford mid-way up; see how the gill is ushered through the structure and the corresponding wall-stiles (neither relevant to ramblers) and sheep creeps, the left-hand one an unusual arched form with original blocking stone in situ. After the hand-gate exit the lane. 5 Either follow Broadslack Beck up through the bracken and outcropping, quite tricky and no path, onto Tail Crag spur ridge or 6, stick with the Long Mire Beck, following the turf trail over the hause to merge with the Park Head Road, bearing up the quarry incline, as with route 1. A further link approach starts at the Kiln Bank Cross hause at the head of the Dunnerdale Beck valley, 7 again following the Park Head Road green-way to the Caw slate mine incline.

The Summit

The perfect summit, but for the imposition of a now redundant white concrete triangulation pillar. Redundant, except in a strong breeze when seeking a steady camera shot of the classic view to the Scafells.

Safe Descents

There are crags on all fronts, the most notable Goat Crags on the blunt western end, so sticking to a path is important. If heading for the Duddon, aim for the Park Head Road, though be watchful for the right-hand fork some 45 metres down the north slope. This leads into a grassy rake and down to the slate mine, bear left with the incline. The broken southern slope is pathless, outcrops and later bracken hampering progress down by Broadslack Beck to join the Long Mire bridleway, leading into the green lane and the road at Stephenson Ground.

Ridge Routes to...

STICKLE PIKE   DESCENT *990ft*   ASCENT *490ft*   2.3 miles

Heed the advice on descent to Park Head Road via Caw slate mine (see *Safe Descents*), then keep with the track SSW over Brock Barrow hause to the open road at Kiln Bank Cross, following the clear path heading up the bank in the same direction, climbing to the compact summit.

WALNA SCAR   DESCENT *190ft*   ASCENT *280ft*   2.5 miles

There are two options. Firstly follow the ridge NE to meet the bridle-path emerging from the head of the Lickle valley. Either follow its continuation, passing below the Walna Scar Quarries to join the Walna Scar Road up to the pass, or link with the ascent of White Maiden from the vicinity of Natty Bridge, via Caw Moss (consult route **3** Walna Scar, page 190).

The Duddon from the drove-way

PANORAMA

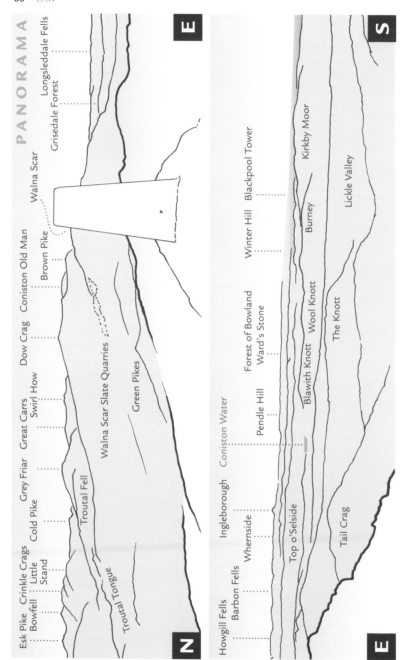

E

Longsleddale Fells
Grisedale Forest
Walna Scar
Brown Pike
Coniston Old Man
Dow Crag
Swirl How
Great Carrs
Grey Friar
Cold Pike
Little Stand
Crinkle Crags
Bowfell
Esk Pike

Walna Scar Slate Quarries
Green Pikes
Troutal Fell
Troutal Tongue

N

S

Kirkby Moor
Blackpool Tower
Winter Hill
Burney
Lickle Valley
Ward's Stone
Forest of Bowland
Wool Knott
Blawith Knott
The Knott
Pendle Hill
Coniston Water
Top o'Selside
Ingleborough
Whernside
Tail Crag
Barbon Fells
Howgill Fells

E

1: Hard Knott

CONISTON OLD MAN 6

As life turns, fads and fashions change, but not so readily mountains. The old allure lingers, such distinguished fells as the Old Man of Coniston will have laid claim to regular, even daily, visits from time immemorial. The compulsion to climb the long slate staircase is always rewarded by a life-enhancing majestic sensation of being on top of a worthier world, the industrial wasteland of mineral and slate extraction falling away as eyes are raised to a sumptuous panorama of mountain Lakeland. Yet the holy grail of the Old Man is but the tailpiece of a wonderful ridge parade which has its actual culmination a little under two miles further north upon Swirl How. Hence the natural tendency for walkers to execute a clockwise horseshoe from Coniston, ending with the descent from Wetherlam back into the Coppermines valley. Mercifully the intrinsic qualities of the eastern combes leading down to the village of Coniston have not been spoilt by stone extraction. In fact there is much to intrigue in what remains of the workings.

Visitors curious to know more about the extractive history of the valley should consult Eric G. Holland's *Coniston Copper Mines, a field guide* and for greater depth his *Coniston Copper – a history*, both published by Cicerone Press.

803 *metres*   2,635 *feet*

All maps worth their salt declare this to be the Old Man of Coniston, though colloquially known as Coniston Old Man. Harry Griffin called it the 'kindly monarch' appropriate as the fell-name literally meant 'high boundary stone' for a small Viking kingdom centred upon Coniston Water. John Ruskin took daily delight in the view of the Old Man from his home across the lake *(shown left)*. One of the most important influences advancing Victorian thought, Ruskin's advocacy of the excellence of this mountain prospect was in kilter with contemporary taste. He felt that mountains are the beginning and end of all that is truly scenic; pilgrims to Brantwood will see no cause to doubt his judgement.

There are actually three principal routes to the top, the ridge-end situation giving more scope for tortuous trails than many walkers realise.

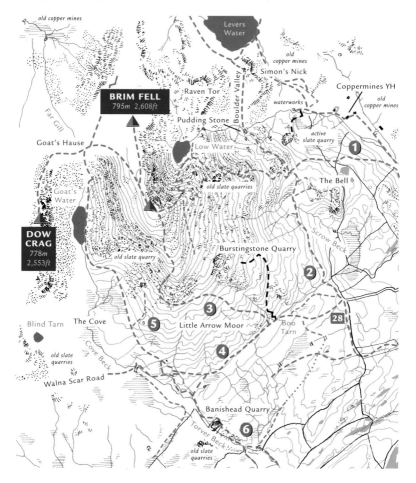

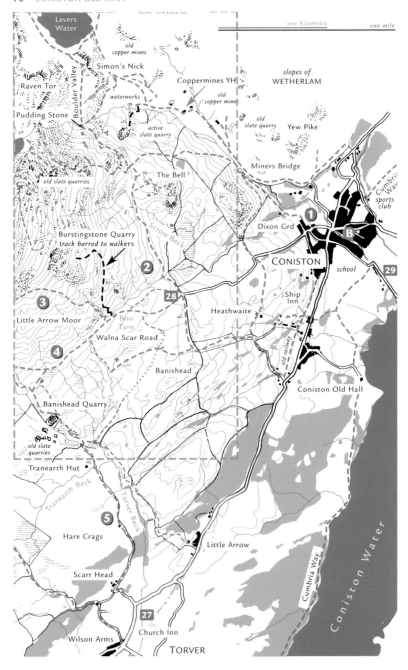

MAP OVERLEAF

Levers Water

one kilometre   one mile

old copper mines

Simon's Nick

Raven Tor

Coppermines YH

slopes of WETHERLAM

waterworks

Pudding Stone

old copper mine

old slate quarry

Yew Pike

active slate quarry

The Bell

Miners Bridge

old slate quarries

Cumbria Way

sports club

Scrow Beck

Dixon Grd

1

B

Burstingstone Quarry
track barred to walkers

2

CONISTON

school

29

3

28

Ship Inn

Little Arrow Moor

Boo Tarn

Heathwaite

4

Walna Scar Road

Banishead

old railway

Banishead Quarry

Coniston Old Hall

old slate quarries

Tranearth Hut

Tranearth Beck

Torver Beck

5

Hare Crags

Little Arrow

Scarr Head

Cumbria Way

Coniston Water

27

Church Inn

Wilson Arms

TORVER

Coniston is a service centre village, rare in Lakeland, where local and visitor alike can find most things to meet their needs: from launch cruises to lunch courses, micro-brewing to cultural exhibition – the principal attraction being the Ruskin Museum, quite the most absorbing of its kind. Learn not just the robust detail of an agrarian and industrial heritage, but witness the influence of great people on the locality, from John Ruskin to Donald Campbell. Come and be inspired!

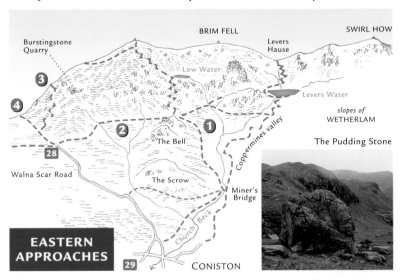

Invariably parties of walkers traipse up the fell direct **1|2** the discerning, in their ones and twos, find the best of the fell by starting from the Walna Scar Road, either **3** winding up the whaleback south ridge above Burstingstone, or from the west by the Cove and Goat's Hause **4**.

ASCENT *from Coniston*

1 From the bridge in the middle of the village, either take the road past the Black Bull (and I do mean pass, no time for Old Man Bitter now!) and the Ruskin Museum, rising to become an open track with Church Beck close left. Or, cross the bridge by Barclays Bank, rising with the lane turning right behind the Sun Hotel to a gate at Dixon Ground, an open path advancing to a kissing-gate, now with Church Beck close right. At the gate on Miner's Bridge the two routes can come together. Keep to the south bank, soon to climb diagonally up the slope via hand-gates, with open views of the extensive spoil and remaining buildings of the Coppermines valley over to the right (including the youth hostel). Reaching the saddle between the Bell and the main fell, a track from the Walna Scar Road fell-gate is joined **2**. Bear up the main ascending quarrymen's track, toil up, passing various facets of the Saddlestone quarry working platforms with track, winding gear and ruined tooling sheds: stark reminders of hard toil of another age. The massive Saddle-stone Quarry (fenced to ward off casual visitations) has an eerie interior, with much loose rock *(see right)*. The nature of the slate being inferior to the regular planes of Snowdonian slate, the level of development was mercifully nowhere near as great. Arrival at Low Water gives an excuse to pause before tackling the final narrow winding quarry-engineered path up the northern slope. The concentrated use means that, for all the repair work undertaken, loose slate continues to give discomfort.

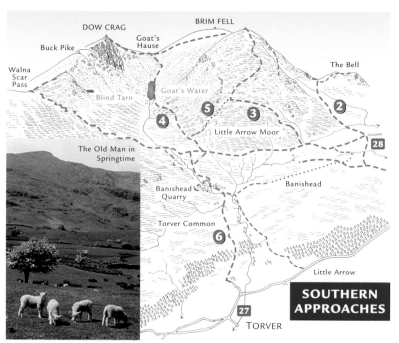

ASCENT *from the Walna Scar Road fell-gate and Torver*

One wonders how many walkers come to Coniston, set on the Old Man, park down Lakes Road and flog up the narrow Walna Scar Road to reach the fell-gate and look in dismay – not at the massive bulk of the fell ahead, but rather at the large car parking area before them. Be consoled, their hike is a necessary warm-up for the rigours ahead! Immediately two options are apparent. **2** Go right along the open track to link with the direct route, an opportunity to visit the top of the Bell *(see page 6)*, a mini-mountain and a superb situation, offering an intimate view of the Coppermines valley and one objective if mist threatens to spoil the day.

3 Quite the better option follows the Walna Scar Road (an open cart-track) westward. Pass the foot of the Burstingstone Quarry track: the quarry is still occasionally active, hence the metal barrier. See a footpath sign directing right for the Old Man. This climbs the bank, drifting leftward onto a shoulder of Little Arrow Moor. An older path runs on across the eastern slope above the quarry, but this has fallen from favour and is now rarely used. The popular path comes close to the edge, overlooking the Cove, then bears up right onto the upper ridge with no hazards. **4** Alternatively, continue with the Walna Scar track, which rises through two rock cuttings to branch right up steps onto a clear, part-pitched path traversing into the Cove. **5** An old green path can be followed right up by a ruin; this was originally an access to the old quarries high up on the SW slope of the Old Man. Branch up the pathless slope from the ruin to the skyline to join the Little Arrow Moor path, just where it hits the edge. Most walkers continue with the path up the Cove, over the Goat Crag rock step and along the eastern shore of Goat's Water. The pitched path winds up to Goat's Hause depression, then swings naturally up right to the summit. The path is never in doubt - more's the pity, inevitable erosion all too apparent. This route is most frequently used as an easy descent to save jaded knees.

6 From Torver, park at the Church Hall (£1 donation requested) next to St Luke's and the Church House Inn, or at the road-end GR 285945. Follow the lane up by Scarr Head, entering a gated bridle-lane signed to Walna Scar. Pass ruined barns, the track signed Tranearth. Cross a concrete bridge, with Tranearth Climbers' Hut over to left. Tranearth means 'ground frequented by great cranes', now only found on continental Europe: it is a cousin of the grey heron. Continue to a hand-gate through sheep handling pens to another gate and over the wooden bridge. Keep to the main track, up through the slate tips to swing round the fenced Banishead quarry. At the western end Torver Beck falls into the pool *(see right)* at the base of the quarry and mysteriously soaks away via a cave. The route ascends the bracken bank, with several green-ways to choose from, to merge with the Walna Scar track.

Coniston village and lake looking towards the distant Pennines, from the south ridge

The Summit

The drystone viewing platform and cairn used to be a handsome edifice, twice its present height, is now depleted and in need of a serious face-lift. The stone-built OS column affords an ideal leaning post to stand awestruck. The profound drop beneath your feet into the hanging valley of Low Water puts you in cloud-nine space. This is the best view in the Coniston group: across the Coppermines valley to Wetherlam backed by ridge after ridge of wonderful fells; half-left the Scafells appear with considerable stature. Wander left to get a face-on perspective on Dow Crag. The ridge-edge location gives a sense of isolation and finality, the fells one way, the wooded lowlands about Coniston Water to the sea southward. Doubtless people will also look down Morecambe Bay and spot the square block of Heysham Power Station and stretch their gaze to Blackpool Tower. But the majority, having climbed this impressive height, will feel on top of the world and thankful that they committed themselves to the climb, the pain evaporating the instant the brink is calmly gained.

SLIGHT SIDE
SCAFELL
SCAFELL PIKE
BROAD CRAG
ILL CRAG
GREY FRIAR
GREAT END
ESK PIKE
BOWFELL
CRINKLE CRAGS
BRIM FELL

A scene re-enacted thousands of times each year, as walkers rest, consume a snack, happily chatter and gaze out from this most wonderful viewpoint.

Safe Descents

Wind is always a nuisance and on occasion a real danger on the fells. Prevailing south-westerlies encourage walkers to seek the shelter of the popular slate staircase down by Low Water, heading directly for Church Beck, while the most pleasant descent is without question that by Goat's Water on the path heading NW from the summit. This curves down to the broad saddle of Goat's Hause, turn due S down the pitched path to glance by the shores of Goat's Water, venturing on down the Cove to meet the Walna Scar Road; turn left for Coniston, or straight on, by Banishead quarry, for Torver.

Low Water and Wetherlam from the summit

Ridge Routes to...

BRIM FELL   DESCENT 190*ft*   ASCENT 280*ft*   0.5 miles

There are no logs on the ridge, but the walk to Brim Fell is as easy as falling off one. The one concern – keep the steep ground of the corrie a comfortable distance to the right, I don't want you to fall off that either. Take care you are not drawn down the popular path NW to Goat's Hause, an easy error. The ridge broadens, as does the path, as it advances north to the large solitary cairn.

DOW CRAG   DESCENT 190*ft*   ASCENT 280*ft*   0.8 miles

A exciting walk linking two neighbourly summits. The very evident path leads NW, curving down to Goat's Hause. Climb naturally round the scarp W, turning to S on the climb to the magnificent summit bastion.

Looking back to the summit from the ridge path to Brim Fell

PANORAMA

E

Coniston Water
Fell Head
Whinfell Beacon
Claife Heights
Windermere
Coniston
The Bell
Grey Crag
Tarn Hows
Black Fell
Yew Pike
Sweeten Crag
Church Beck
Youth Hostel
Burlington's Quarry
Hole Rake
Leverswater Beck
Coppermines Valley
Holme Fell
Low Water
Boulder Valley
Lad Stones
Red Dell
Levers Water
Wetherlam
Black Sails
Raven Tor
Stickle Tarn

1 2 3 4 5 6 7 8 9 10 11 12 13 14 15 16 17 18 19 20 21 22 23 24 25 26 27 28 29 30 31

N

1: Skiddaw Little Man 2: Swirl How
3: Lonscale Fell 4: High Raise
5: Great How Crags 6: Swirl Hause
7: Harrison Stickle 8: Blencathra
9: Clough Head 10: Great Dodd
11: Helvellyn 12: Nethermost Pike
13: Dollywaggon Pike 14: Grisedale Hause
15: Fairfield 16: Great Rigg 17: Hart Crag 18: Heron Pike 19: Dove Crag
20: High Pike 21: Little Hart Crag 22: Rampsgill Head 23: Red Screes 24: Kidsty Pike 25: High Street
26: Thornthwaite Crag 27: Froswick 28: Ill Bell 29: Kentmere Pike 30: Wansfell Pike 31: Tarn Crag

S

Irish Sea
Blawith Knott
Torver
Blackpool
Winter Hill
Morecambe Bay
Top o'Selside
Peel Island
Grisedale Forest
Forest of Bowland
Ward's Stone
Ingleborough
Windermere
Brantwood

E

The Calf
Baugh Fell
Hawkshead
Coniston Moor
Coniston Water

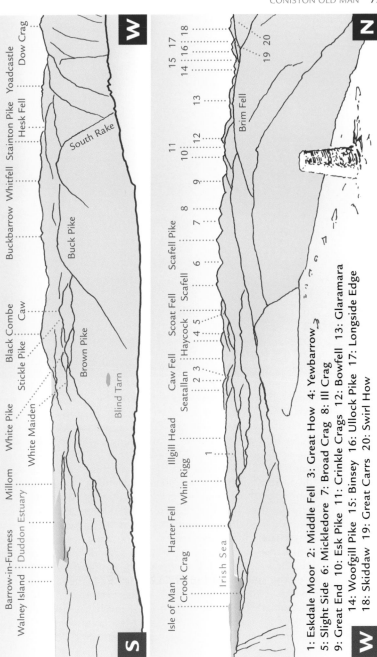

S

W

Barrow-in-Furness — Millom — White Pike — Black Combe — Buckbarrow — Whitfell — Stainton Pike — Yoadcastle

Walney Island — Duddon Estuary — Stickle Pike — Caw — Hesk Fell — Dow Crag

White Maiden

South Rake

Brown Pike — Buck Pike

Blind Tarn

N

W

Isle of Man — Harter Fell — Illgill Head — Caw Fell — Scoat Fell — Scafell Pike

Crook Crag — Whin Rigg — Seatallan — Haycock — Scafell

Brim Fell

Irish Sea

1: Eskdale Moor 2: Middle Fell 3: Great How 4: Yewbarrow
5: Slight Side 6: Mickledore 7: Broad Crag 8: Ill Crag
9: Great End 10: Esk Pike 11: Crinkle Crags 12: Bowfell 13: Glaramara
14: Woofgill Pike 15: Binsey 16: Ullock Pike 17: Longside Edge
18: Skiddaw 19: Great Carrs 20: Swirl How

DOW CRAG

One of the finest fells in the Lake District: revered by rock climbers and fellwalkers alike. Good to look at, good to stand upon, good to wander over, a superb climb whatever your capacity or approach. Granted that from the Duddon all it offers is bulk, a tantalising peaked summit with no obvious line of direct ascent, but from the east it's a different matter: whether upon the Old Man *(see above)*, approaching up the Cove, or more distantly from Coniston Water, comprehend a real mountain, dominated by one absolutely massive crag, its buttresses and gullies on a par with Scafell, that humble the bold and awe-strike the timid. The South Rake, the simplest of scambles, gives fellwalkers their most intimate view of the cliff. Otherwise walkers must be content to cautiously admire the wild precipice from a safe distance along its fearsome edge. Dow Crag is most commonly approached either via Goat's Hause or the summit of the Walna Scar Road, the latter northbound ridge makes two impressive bink steps, over Brown and Buck Pikes. Cradled beneath them Blind Tarn is as lovely a crystal pool as nature can bestow. By contrast, Goat's Water has an altogether darker feel, with crags and scree pressing down upon its steely chilled waters.

778 metres   *2,553 feet*

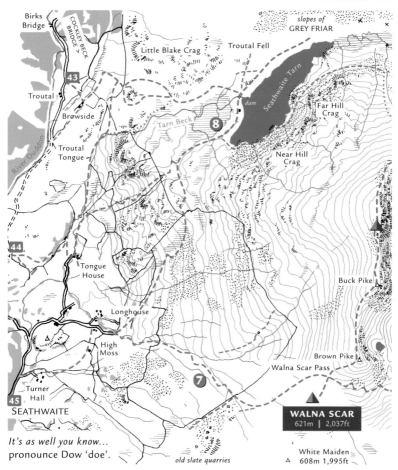

It's as well you know...
pronounce Dow 'doe'.

old slate quarries

ASCENT *from Coniston via Walna Scar Road*

The approach off the Walna Scar Road via the Cove, entering the great amphitheatre beneath the famous crag, is one of great drama and excitement, but is hidden and not suspected from the start. The aura of climbers past lends this mountain arena a special reverence and respect.

1 Start from the fell-gate car parking, follow the open track west, passing the tiny rush-filled Boo Tarn. To the left swathes of bracken shield the common, where lie remnant stones from the Bronze Age agrarian colonisation of this upland. The track begins to climb, winding through two rock cuttings, the latter-day work of slate quarrymen. Over the span of many centuries travellers have had no cause to alter the course of this ancient route-way. Watch for the obvious pitched steps right, leading off

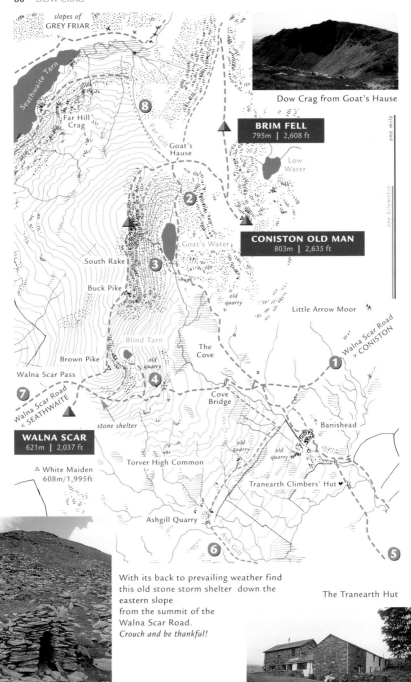

slopes of
GREY FRIAR

Seathwaite Tarn

Far Hill
Crag

Goat's
Hause

8

Dow Crag from Goat's Hause

BRIM FELL
795m | 2,608 ft

Low
Water

2

Goat's Water

CONISTON OLD MAN
803m | 2,635 ft

South Rake

3

Buck Pike

old
quarry

Little Arrow Moor

Blind Tarn

The
Cove

Walna Scar Road
> CONISTON

Brown Pike

old
quarry

4

Walna Scar Pass

7

Walna Scar Road
< SEATHWAITE

Cove
Bridge

1

Banishead

stone shelter

WALNA SCAR
621m | 2,037 ft

old
quarry

old
quarry

△ White Maiden
608m/1,995ft

Torver High Common

Tranearth Climbers' Hut

Ashgill Quarry

Ash Gill

6

5

one mile

one kilometre

With its back to prevailing weather find
this old stone storm shelter down the
eastern slope
from the summit of the
Walna Scar Road.
Crouch and be thankful!

The Tranearth Hut

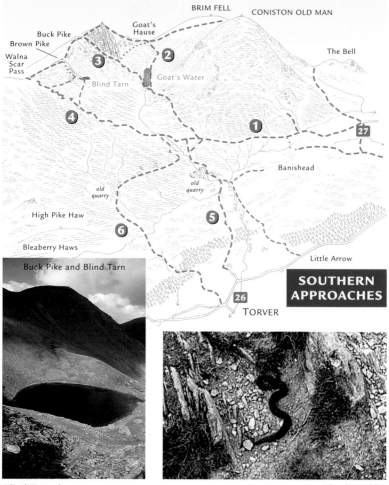

BRIM FELL
CONISTON OLD MAN
Goat's
Hause
Buck Pike
Brown Pike
Walna
Scar
Pass
③
②
The Bell
Blind Tarn
Goat's Water
④
①
27
Banishead
old
quarry
old
quarry
High Pike Haw
⑤
⑥
Bleaberry Haws
Little Arrow
Buck Pike and Blind Tarn

SOUTHERN APPROACHES

26
TORVER

Blind Tarn slate quarry
in the foreground

A rare encounter with a live adder
- unravelling for a quick exit

the track 180 metres short of Cove Bridge – the present structure built to
serve the Blind Tarn slate quarry. When walking with my life-long friend
Rodney Busby in July, we spotted an adder coiled up on the path.
Normally they feel walkers' vibrations and scuttle off before you even see
them. This one lingered long enough for me to down my rucksack and
swiftly wield my camera for a recording shot. A digital camera, which
needs to wake up its pixels, would have missed the moment. Not only did
I get the photo but it gave us the benefit of a passing hiss... becoming
'hiss'tory in the blink of an eye.

The path mounts a rock step beneath Goat Crag and advances to Goat's Water. **2** The setting is wonderfully wild, not a tree or a shrub in sight, just boulders and coarse scree bearing down into the dark waters. To meet the demands of a regular clientele the path has been pitched, drawing up to the saddle at the head of the combe. Go left, turning from west to south as the worn ridge path climbs steadily to the final, triumphant summit castle.

3 If the weather is suitable and your energy levels up to form, serious consideration should be given to climbing South Rake, it is the fellwalker's one chance to get really close to Dow Crag. Ford the outflowing beck from Goat's Water, passing giant boulders. The scree above is not pleasant, to be honest it's horrid, but there's no choice. The path climbs up to the foot of Great Gully, with the blue stretcher box down to the right. A contouring sheep trod can be followed right beneath the crag to Goat's Hause. Enter South Rake by bearing up left, scramble by the entrance to Easy Gully, onto the rough ledges. The Rake is obvious, there is no sense of entering a deep cleft or forbidding gully, just a scrambly open weakness that, yes, has its loose stuff, but far more of the firm 'hand-holdy' stuff that lends confidence and ensures steady progress. The outward views down to the tarn and across the blank side of the Old Man are fabulous, but most impressive are the near buttresses. Nonetheless, the rake is no place for ordinary fellwalking types in bad weather. To enjoy it, do it on a sunny day, take your time and stop often, it is fun. The top comes sooner than may be expected; chuffed with yourself, you'll relish grappling with the summit when at last it arrives.

4 For the simplest ascent stick with the Walna Scar Road to the top of the pass, bear right onto the rising ridge, via the strategic cairns on Brown and Buck Pikes. A visit to Blind Tarn is a delectable addition, using the old quarry green-way. The tarn will perplex, there being only a soakaway pool and no sign of an escaping gill, not even tell-tale rushes. Explore the quarries and use a narrow trod traversing from the upper quarry back to the track close to the stone shelter. There are two lines of approach to the Walna Scar Road from Torver *(see page 81)*. **5** The usual route, via Tranearth and Banishead quarry, and by starting at the Wilson Arms. **6** This follows the footpath lane rising through woodland and up an old trackway onto the fell via gates and stiles leading to Ashgill quarry. Traverse right to rise on an old path by Torver Beck to Cove Bridge.

Coniston Old Man from the
outflow soakaway of Blind Tarn

Easy Gully

South Rake

Great Gully

Goat's Hause traverse

scree paths to crag

boulder cave

path from tarn outflow

View up Great Gully

Dow Crag from the eastern shore of Goat's Water

(above) The amazing view of Dow Crag from midway up South Rake; see the blue mountain rescue stretcher box at the base of the cliff.

(left) Coniston Old Man from South Rake

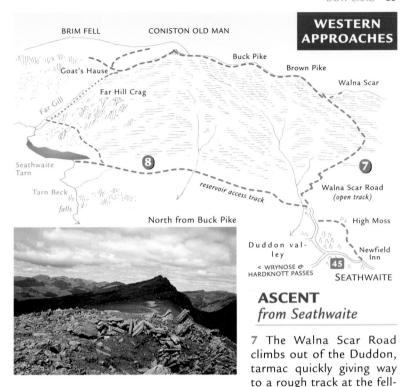

BRIM FELL   CONISTON OLD MAN

Goat's Hause

Buck Pike

Brown Pike

Walna Scar

Far Hill Crag

Far Gill

8

7

Seathwaite Tarn

Tarn Beck

falls

reservoir access track

Walna Scar Road (open track)

North from Buck Pike

High Moss

Duddon valley

Newfield Inn

< WRYNOSE & HARDKNOTT PASSES

45

SEATHWAITE

ASCENT
from Seathwaite

7 The Walna Scar Road climbs out of the Duddon, tarmac quickly giving way to a rough track at the fell-gate. Popular with pedal and petrol bikers, the 'road' provides a straightforward, efficient means of getting onto the Dow Crag ridge. **8** The track begins as the gated reservoir access track bound for Seathwaite Tarn, a water supply for the lower Furness area. This traverses the lower western slopes; branch right, short of the dam, joining a path which draws across the fell-side, passing a measuring gauge, beneath Near and Far Hill Crags. The path peters out when opposite Blake Rigg Crag; ascend with Far Gill to Goat's Hause.

From Coniston Old Man south ridge

BUCK PIKE   DOW CRAG

North along the summit ridge

The Summit

There are summits and there are summits: Brim Fell needs a cairn, Dow Crag doesn't. There's no room for one thing. The irregular battlement of the summit bastion *(see right, the northern aspect)*, like a Roman altar, has a focus. I count this among the best summits in the Lakes, an easy scramble on and off, north and south... but oh the horrors if you lurch east! The view down the cliff is utterly breathtaking: there are few summits with quite this sense of the precipitous. Southward along the edge are further glimpses down the face from the high brow; peer down Easy and Great Gullies *(below right)* to marvel at the void. The ridge path runs besides the remains of a wall, originally constructed to stop sheep from venturing onto the cliff. The lack of such protection means it is not uncommon to see Herdwick engage in goat-like antics on amazing ledges. I witnessed a ewe and lamb work their way down, stepping from ledge to ledge, engrossed in grazing; inevitably they must get to a point where they either fall or successfully unravel their way back up the cliff *(pick them out, below left)*. The names Goat's Water and Buck Pike testify to a lost population of wild goats.

ewe & lamb

Safe Descents

For all the eastern scarp threatens, especially with a stiff southwesterly blowing, the walker can make safe haven more readily from this top than many another. The simple reality is that if you follow the ridge S, stepping down first from Buck Pike, then Brown Pike, the summit of the Walna Scar Road (open track) is sure to be found. Then either go right for Seathwaite in the Duddon (2.3 miles), or left for Coniston (3.3 miles). It's a similar story should you trek N, for the ridge naturally declines to the broad saddle of Goat's Hause from where a pitched path leads S down by Goat's Water. An obvious continuation leads via a rock step at Goat Crag, down the Cove, again to meet the Walna Scar Road, though this time Coniston will be your destination (2 miles), the Duddon being uphill and over the pass. The steeper slope N from Goat's Hause has no real dangers, but the terrain to the reservoir track is rougher and the distance to Seathwaite just that bit greater (4.2 miles).

Ridge Routes to...

BRIM FELL   DESCENT 423 ft   ASCENT 478 ft   0.7 miles
CONISTON OLD MAN   DESCENT 423 ft   ASCENT 510 ft   1 mile

Climb carefully down the N side of the summit outcrop, descend with the ridge path to the broad depression of Goat's Hause. The main continuing path curves up with a right-hand bias; for Brim Fell branch off at will up the predominantly grassy slope; for the Old Man stick with the trade route. In mist, be aware, the steepest ground lies to the east.

WALNA SCAR   DESCENT 585 ft   ASCENT 72 ft   1 mile

Follow the ridge S, via Buck and Brown Pikes, down to the Walna Scar track; the modest summit and cairn lie at the top of the first rise beyond.

Swirl How and Brim Fell across the saddle of Goat's Hause from the north ridge

P A N O R A M A

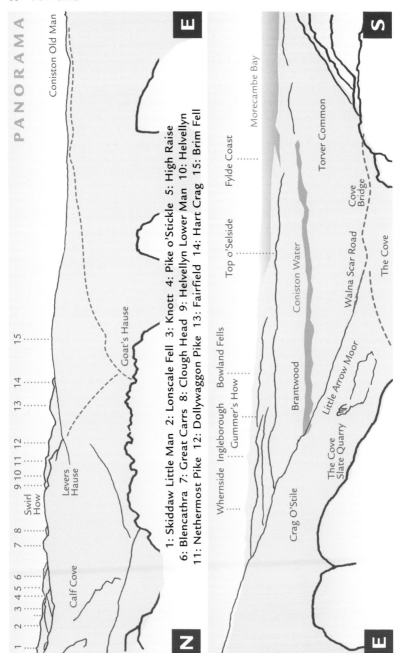

Coniston Old Man

Goat's Hause

15 14 13 12 9 10 11 8 7 6 5 4 3 2 1

Swirl How

Levers Hause

Calf Cove

N

1: Skiddaw Little Man 2: Lonscale Fell 3: Knott 4: Pike o'Stickle 5: High Raise
6: Blencathra 7: Great Carrs 8: Clough Head 9: Helvellyn Lower Man 10: Helvellyn
11: Nethermost Pike 12: Dollywaggon Pike 13: Fairfield 14: Hart Crag 15: Brim Fell

E

Morecambe Bay

Fylde Coast

Top o'Selside

Torver Common

Cove Bridge

The Cove

Walna Scar Road

Coniston Water

Little Arrow Moor

Brantwood

The Cove Slate Quarry

Whernside Ingleborough Bowland Fells

Gummer's How

Crag O'Stile

E

S

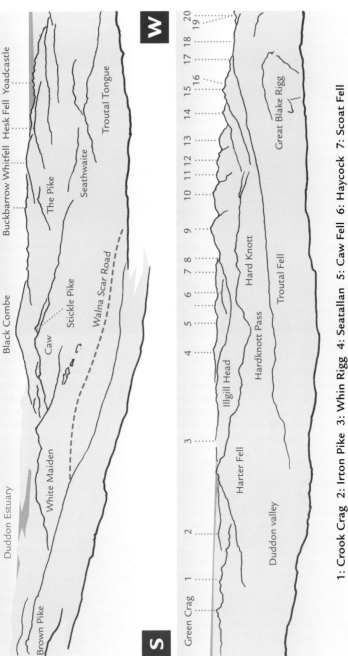

1: Crook Crag 2: Irton Pike 3: Whin Rigg 4: Seatallan 5: Caw Fell 6: Haycock 7: Scoat Fell
8: Slight Side 9: Scafell 10: Scafell Pike 11: Broad Crag 12: Ill Crag 13: Great End 14: Esk Pike
15: Bowfell 16: Crinkle Crags 17: Grey Friar 18: Glaramara 19: Carl Side 20: Skiddaw

GREAT CARRS   8

A curving crescendo ridge, born in the meadows of Little Langdale, culminating upon the peaks of Great Carrs and Swirl How *(see above and below)*. Forming the bridgehead with the Mid-Western Fells on Wrynose Pass, this ridge steps purposefully up by Rough Crags, Wet Side Edge and Little Carrs, and is the focus of most ascents. Walks begun from the Wrynose Pass involve just 1,295ft/395m of ascent; the saving is compromised when any walk is extended; circular expeditions are limited: Swirl How and Grey Friar can only be considered in a natural backtracking plan. From Wrynose Bottom the fell is guarded by a high rim of crags dominated by Hellgill Pike. To visit this follow a tough off-beat clamber up the west side of Hell Gill. The lonely upper reaches of the Greenburn Beck valley, a glacial hollow filled with boulders and marsh, is the least attractive approach. Most walkers wisely settle for Swirl Hause and Prison Band, rather than slog up the excessively steep grass slope of Broad Slack.

SWIRL HOW   GREAT CARRS

From Wet Side Edge

788 *metres*   2,585 *feet*

The fell-name is a contraction
of the British 'carreg', and is
descriptive of the great
rock-wall at the head of
Greenburn Beck
valley.

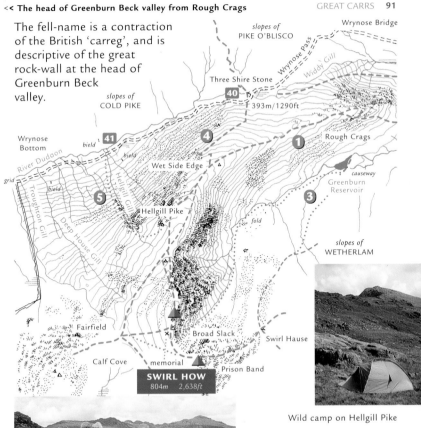

Wild camp on Hellgill Pike

Walkers consider their map from the
ridge above Rough Crags

Scafell and Little Stand
from the head of Hell Gill

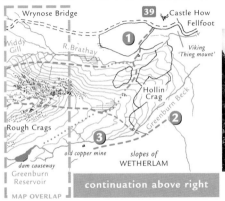

continuation above right

MAP OVERLAP

(top) The Langdale Pikes from Hollin Crag
(middle) Greenburn Tarn dam causeway

ASCENT *from Little Langdale*

There are two ways onto the Rough Crags ridge, the quicker begins from above Fellfoot Farm. **1** Immediately above Castle How find a recessed gate/stile on the left. Follow the track with a wall left, go through the next gate, slip over the facing bank, passing a guide cairn, to ford the infant River Brathay. Climb the steep bank ahead, between irregular walled enclosures; passing the distinctive rocks on Hollin Crag, traverse right, up the easy ridge. **2** This lowest section of the ridge can be gained from the old Greenburn mine access track. Rise from a footbridge over Greenburn Beck, situated directly right after the intake wall gate at GR 295023. The track can either be joined from Fellfoot via Bridge End or, more commonly, from the vicinity of Slater Bridge via the lane by High Hall Garth. The ridge path angles up the left side of Rough Crags above Greenburn Tarn, progressing steadily by Wet Side Edge which is actually quite dry. The path from Wrynose enters from the right at a prominent cairn; either keep with the main path or slant

Great Carrs rising from Little Langdale Tarn

left to follow the true ridge path climbing more steeply up Little Carrs. **3** The mine access track leads not only to remains of the old copper mine, but along the dwindling trod into the wild corrie beyond Greenburn Tarn, aiming for either Swirl Hause (path) or Broad Slack (no path). Soggy ground culminates in a painfully steep grass slope and the remains of a Hercules bomber's fuselage litters the scree.*(Above)* a memorial cross and cairn are located a few yards down the west slope from the lip of Broad Slack at GR 270007. The Merlin engine stands outside the Ruskin Museum in Coniston, where an account of the 1944 accident is given.

ASCENT *from Wrynose Pass and Bottom*

The Wrynose Pass is oh so tempting. **4** A high-level walk that can start at 393m/1,295ft and involve only the same height gain upon a simple ridge is hard to ignore. As an exclusive there-and-back route to the top of Great Carrs, it is just fine. There are two parking areas, though only one regular path onto the ridge, beginning from the actual top of the pass. Glance at the huge specimen erratic close left as you climb just west of south onto the ridge. A large cairn marks the point of arrival on the ridge-top; commit its characteristics to memory for your return, in case mist descends with you; you'll not wish to drift down the too far!

The serpentine road descends west from the pass into Wrynose Bottom. Notice two short lengths of wall on the fellside, these are old shelter bields for sheep. **5** This is one of those climbs that make sense on the map and on the ground in fair weather, but strangely shows little or no sign of use. Find room to pull off the open road just west of the footpath, signed on the north bank GR 266023. A cattle rack standing in the vicinity of the starting point, confirming that cattle are being given their chance to graze the lower dale slopes, good news for plant life diversity. The striking cleft of Hell Gill is not a place to fear, unlike its namesake on Bowfell's Band. Keeping to the west side, ascend above the rowans; gain entry into the upper sector of the ravine as it slips through the rock band, passing a small pinnacle. Buzzards wheeled above me during my fell climb, the rare visit of homo sapiens was greeted with disdain. From the higher realms of the gill the views across the valley are quite superb, with Little Stand, Cold Pike and beyond to a grand array of fine fells, including Scafell. As the slope eases one may comfortably drift half-left to climb Hell Gill Pike's cairn peak, sufficiently set aside the main ridge path to enjoy exclusivity for high-level camps. Cross the traversing path bound for the Fairfield saddle and Grey Friar, and climb south up the steepening slope onto the exciting rocky scarp edge to the summit.

Hell Gill. Rowans extend a green
ribbon up the ravine towards Mart Crag,
frequented by crag-nesting buzzards.
A lovely little known fell climb

Hellgill Pike, looking to Harter Fell

Two views from the summit: east to Wetherlam and northeast to Little Langdale

The Summit

A narrow grassy summit ridge, above a fine craggy escarpment, culminates in a small rocky top surmounted by a bedraggled cairn. An impressive spot to rest, peering straight down into the wild hollow of Greenburn. Ahead lies Wetherlam and right Swirl How, while to the north, beyond Little Stand, are the mighty Scafells.

Safe Descents

The main descending ridge, trending from north to east, gives assurance of safe ground towards the Wrynose Pass (1.3 miles) and later, watchful of Rough Crags, down into Little Langdale (Slater Bridge 4 miles).

Ridge Routes to...

GREY FRIAR   DESCENT 423*ft*   ASCENT 300*ft*   0.9 miles

Descend due W, grassy all the way, crossing the Fairfield saddle.

SWIRL HOW   DESCENT 423*ft*   ASCENT 478*ft*   0.3 miles

Follow the curving ridge above Broad Slack *(below)* from S to E.

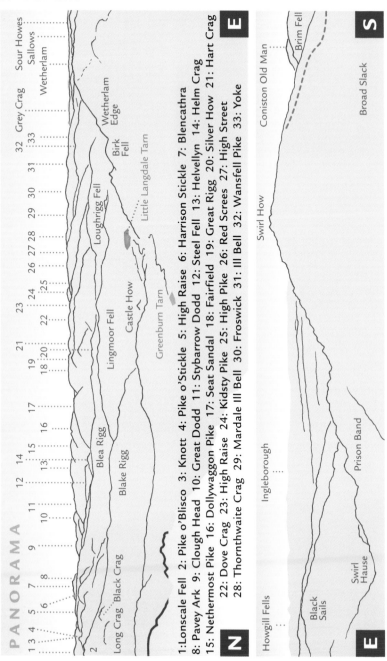

PANORAMA

1: Lonscale Fell 2: Pike o'Blisco 3: Knott 4: Pike o'Stickle 5: High Raise 6: Harrison Stickle 7: Blencathra 8: Pavey Ark 9: Clough Head 10: Great Dodd 11: Stybarrow Dodd 12: Steel Fell 13: Helvellyn 14: Helm Crag 15: Nethermost Pike 16: Dollywaggon Pike 17: Seat Sandal 18: Fairfield 19: Great Rigg 20: Silver How 21: Hart Crag 22: Dove Crag 23: High Raise 24: Kidsty Pike 25: High Pike 26: Red Screes 27: High Street 28: Thornthwaite Crag 29: Mardale Ill Bell 30: Froswick 31: Ill Bell 32: Wansfell Pike 33: Yoke

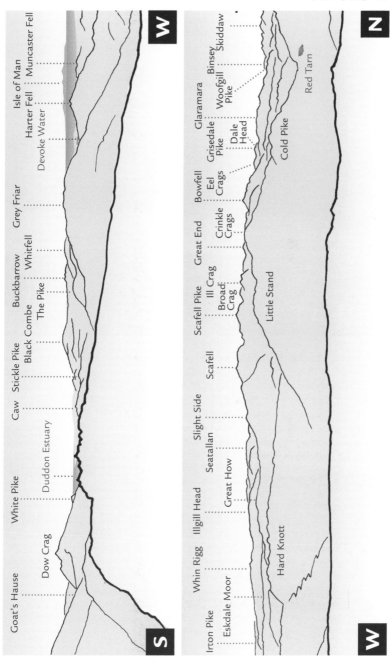

Separated by long tendrils of walled enclosures above the meadows and woods of Hall Dunnerdale *(see above)*, the ground swells to a gentle scarp. Clearly a distinct summit, but for many fellwalkers it is considered nothing more than an intermediate halt, a means to an end, on the approach march to Green Crag from off the Birkerfell Road. But there are enough who appreciate its situation as an end in itself. They know a good view when they see one and, most of all, value the ease with which it may be achieved. The fell-name means 'the monster's head rocks'...

...here be dragons!

ASCENT *from Birkerfell Road*

There are three natural routes to the top. **1** From the point where Freeze Beck flows under the open road a path ascends. After a positive start it falters over marshy ground, then resumes more confidently, passing a heap of anciently gathered stones *(see right)* before rising to the skyline summit cairn, a far more modest assembly of rock. **2** From the cattle grid, where the road emerges onto the open fell, ascend by the wall. As the ridge becomes more apparent, take your leave of the wall, passing above a sheepfold with a fine view towards Caw; angle across the shallow combe to the summit cairn. **3** From Birkerthwaite: for the route to Great Crag consult page 107; thereafter beeline SE up to the summit.

427 *metres*   1,401 *feet*

Green How

consult GREEN CRAG for
the ridge map continuation

GREEN CRAG
489m   1,604ft

High Ground

Ganny
House
Cottage

Birkerthwaite

< ESKDALE
GREEN

Great Crag

Rowantree Beck

webbed feet an asset

Little Crag

Highford Beck

White Crag

5

Birkerfell Road

3

road summit 814 ft
a popular viewpoint

slopes of
YOADCASTLE

ridge path to >
White How

Woodend Pool

Rough Crag

cairn

alcove bield

alcove bield

Woodend Farm

1

6

cairn

2

Ulgra Beck

one kilometre

HESK FELL
476m   1,562ft

Crosbythwaite

Crosby Gill

one mile

alcove bields

HESK FELL

Hazel Head

Baskell Farm

The Pike

ULPHA

Bronze Age cairn above Freeze Beck, one of several in
the area, from a time when the fells were richly wooded

PANORAMA

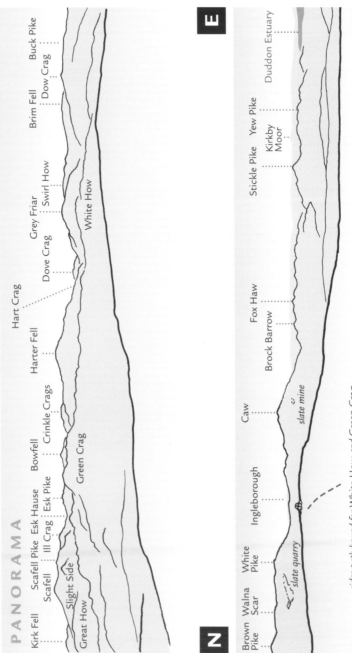

E

Buck Pike
Dow Crag
Brim Fell
Swirl How
Grey Friar
White How
Dove Crag
Hart Crag
Harter Fell
Crinkle Crags
Bowfell
Green Crag
Esk Hause
Scafell Pike   Esk Pike
Ill Crag
Scafell
Slight Side
Kirk Fell
Great How

N

S

Duddon Estuary
Yew Pike
Stickle Pike   Kirkby Moor
Fox Haw
Brock Barrow
Caw
slate mine
Ingleborough
White Pike
Brown   Walna
Pike   Scar
slate quarry

ridge path bound for White How and Green Crag

E

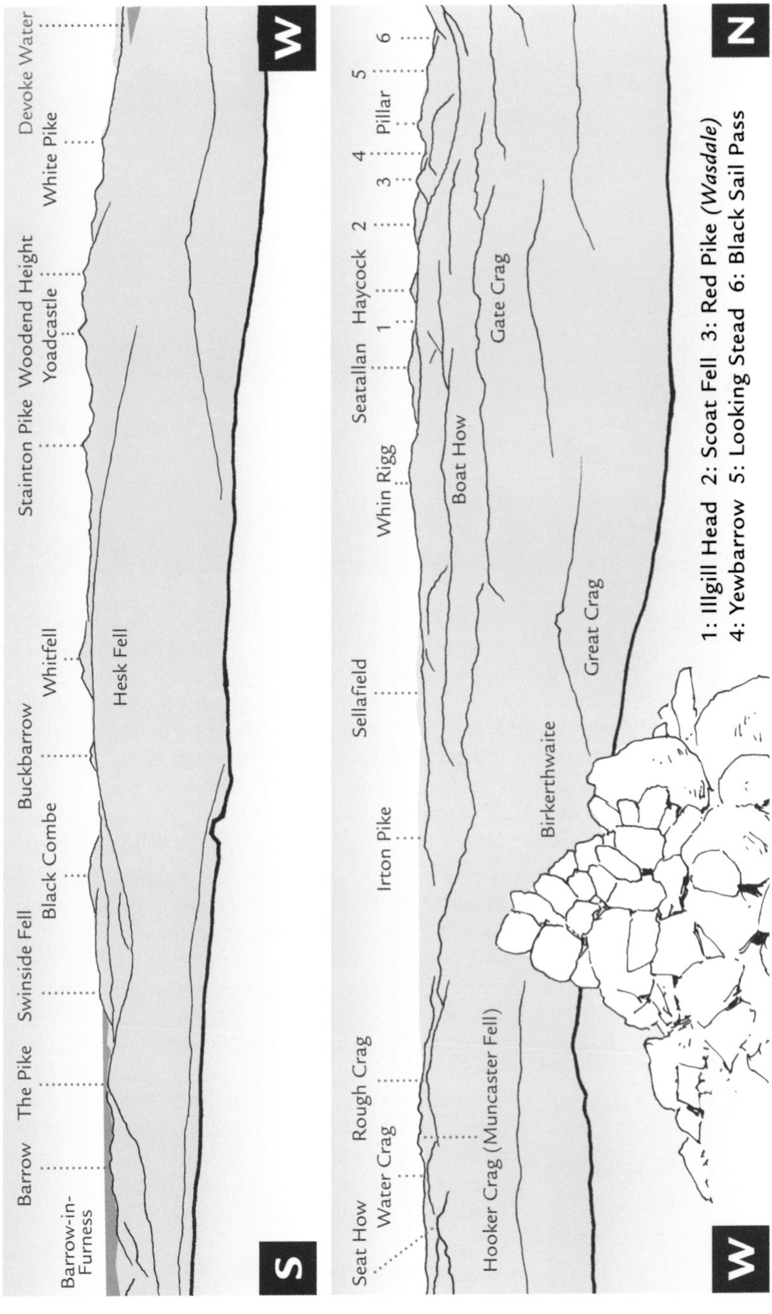

W

Devoke Water
White Pike
Stainton Pike Woodend Height
Yoadcastle
Whitfell
Buckbarrow
Black Combe
Swinside Fell
The Pike
Barrow
Barrow-in-Furness
Hesk Fell
S

N

6
5
Pillar
4
3
Haycock 2
Seatallan 1
Whin Rigg
Sellafield
Irton Pike
Rough Crag Seat How
Water Crag
Hooker Crag (Muncaster Fell)
Birkerthwaite
Boat How
Gate Crag
Great Crag
W

1: Illgill Head 2: Scoat Fell 3: Red Pike (*Wasdale*)
4: Yewbarrow 5: Looking Stead 6: Black Sail Pass

GREEN CRAG 10

Wainwright took the view that this was the end of decent fellwalking south from Eskdale. How you'll know different when you sample the excursions in this guide. But there is no denying the extra special qualities of Green Crag. It holds something of the essence of the Northern Highlands about it: shapely craggy knots elevated from a bleak, boggy moorland. But what makes it different and so superb is dear wooded Eskdale. It is surely only a surly soul who fails to find Eskdale the most exquisite of valleys. When coupled with Green Crag as the high point of a day's walk, one wonders what else life has to offer!

While the regular tourist is content to stroll up Stanley Ghyll by graded paths and stout footbridges to stand before the plunge pool of shady Stanley Force, the fellwalker will revel in the savage beauty of Birker Force, spilling from a rim of craggy ground fringing the upland pastures. The wrench of leaving the verdant tracks and paths of the Duddon and Esk is dispelled by the peace of being removed from the mainstream of fellwalking. The approach from Birkerthwaite over Great Crag best conveys the fell's qualities and character, and may be enjoyed upon a circular expedition including Great Worm Crag – lovely, lonely fellwandering.

Encrusted with lichen, the cairn on White How

489 *metres*   1,604 *feet*

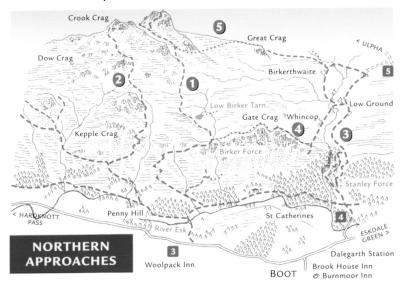

Crook Crag

Great Crag

Dow Crag

Birkerthwaite

< ULPHA

Low Birker Tarn

Low Ground

Gate Crag Whincop

Kepple Crag

Birker Force

Stanley Force

< HARDKNOTT PASS

Penny Hill

St Catherines

River Esk

ESKDALE GREEN >

NORTHERN APPROACHES

Woolpack Inn

BOOT

Dalegarth Station

Brook House Inn & Burnmoor Inn

ASCENT *from the Woolpack Inn & Dalegarth*

Whether starting from the youth hostel or the Woolpack Inn, it is necessary to walk west along the valley road to the lane signed to Penny Hill Farm. Cross the lovely River Esk via Doctor Bridge, there are two options. **1** The more direct route. Go right following the lane and track to Low Birker. Immediately past the house bear up left on the path climbing through the bracken. An early fork right, via a hand-gate, can give access to a rough fell-side as a low down view of the cascading Birker Gill, but this is not a sane route to the scarp top. Preferably keep with the main path, which higher up passes through dense juniper, to a kissing-gate in

the enclosure corner. The peat road, or sled-gate, now begins a quick sequence of zig-zags, then levels to pass a roofless peat store (it would make a splendid camping barn). The sled-gate broaches the moor, missing the best view of Birker Force *(above)*, so make a point of bearing right to find the magnificent downfall, definitely a place to sit for a refreshment break. The old path now embarks upon an altogether bleaker journey skirting marshy ground and rising across the shoulder of a knoll above Low Birker Tarn. A brief descent leads to a long southward

continued on page 106 **>>**

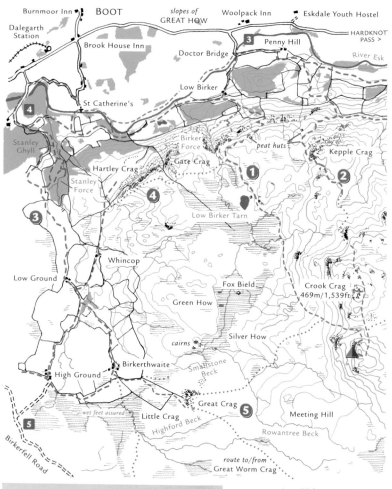

Burnmoor Inn
BOOT
slopes of GREAT HOW
Woolpack Inn
Eskdale Youth Hostel

Dalegarth Station

Brook House Inn

Doctor Bridge

3 Penny Hill

HARDKNOT PASS >

River Esk

Low Birker

4

St Catherine's

Stanley Ghyll

Birker Force

peat huts

Kepple Crag

Gate Crag

1

2

Hartley Crag

Stanley Force

4

Low Birker Tarn

3

Whincop

Low Ground

Fox Bield

Crook Crag 469m/1,539ft

Green How

Silver How

cairns

High Ground

Birkerthwaite

Smallstone Beck

wet feet assured

Little Crag

Highford Beck

Great Crag

5

Meeting Hill

Rowantree Beck

5

Birkerfell Road

route to/from Great Worm Crag

Low Birker peat sled-gate

Eskdale and Scafell from Gate Crag

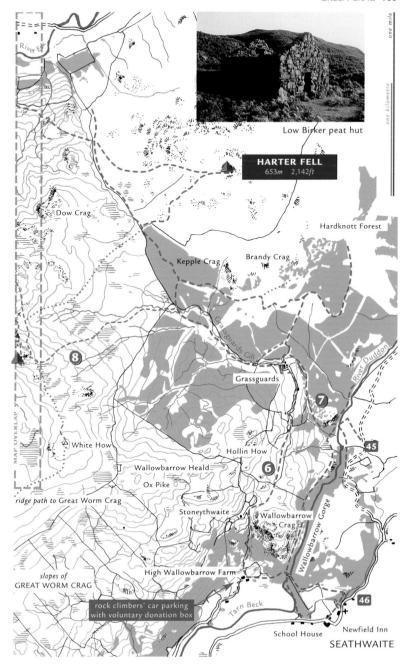

one mile

one kilometre

River

Low Birker peat hut

Dow Crag

HARTER FELL
653m 2,142ft

Hardknott Forest

Kepple Crag

Brandy Crag

Grassguards Gill

8

Grassguards

7

River Duddon

MAP OVERLAP

White How

Hollin How

45

Wallowbarrow Heald

6

Ox Pike

ridge path to Great Worm Crag

Stoneythwaite

Wallowbarrow
Crag

slopes of
GREAT WORM CRAG

High Wallowbarrow Farm

Wallowbarrow Gorge

rock climbers' car parking
with voluntary donation box

Tarn Beck

46

School House

Newfield Inn

SEATHWAITE

slanting traverse. Spot the solitary thorn with its crow's nest... land ahoy! Keep on the path all the way through the light bracken, making for the damp slope rising to the saddle between Crook and Green Crag.

2 Follow the hedged lane ahead towards Penny Hill Farm. A permissive path has been created to avoid unnecessary disturbance to the farmyard; the path is ushered right and left via gates, rejoining the open track leading to a gate and the lonesome pine *(see page 122)*. The track forks, keep right, rising to a gate, then slant left up to a wall; go right to a gate by an old pen. Rising with the wall left, ignore the 'Harter Fell' sign directing left, keep right upon the winding sled-gate, passing three ruined peat stores in rounding Kepple Crag. Slipping over a low saddle between damp combes, head straight up the fell south. Keeping to the right of the prominent outcropping, a path materialises and glances by the lateral ridge-top of Crook Crag, en route for the main saddle, passing the curious one-off boundary stone. Routes **1** and **2** make their own separate ways to the summit.

3 From the Dalegarth Hall car park GR 172002 a lane leads south from the river, crossing the line of the Eskdale Trail – recommended as a means of completing circular walks at scenic dale-floor level. There are two options, either remain with the rising gated lane and subsequent track, or visit the luxuriant environs of Stanley Ghyll, linking to the open track above the woodland. Enter the wooded National Park Access Area via a gate. The popular path leads upstream, crossing three footbridges in the darkly shaded ravine en route to the twelve-metre plunge pool of Stanley Force, spray making paths and woodwork slippery: visitors are warned not to venture beyond, as there is no connection with the open fell. Indeed, during my visit a walker ignored the advice and returned timorously proclaiming the notice to be spot on – erroneously some folks think that such notices are put up for disinformation! Backtrack, ascend the stepped path beside a tiny gill from between the second and third footbridges. The path bends right to descend, with a lovely view ahead of Scafell, framed by the foreground woodland, but at this point

Old boundary stone beneath Green Crag

take the path left on the level, emerging from the wood at a gate. Join the open track – forsaken upon entry to the Access Area – go left, shortly passing through a gate; keep on the green track to the lonely retreat cottage of Low Ground. Cross the stile beside the white-washed dwelling, go left down its access lane. There are three route choices from this lane: either follow the main track to High Ground, still a working farm, where the road is met. Fork left at the conifer spinney, following the footpath direct to Birkerthwaite (useful link to route **5**). Or **4** at the first gate left in a dip, enter an enclosure containing a young deciduous planting. Cross the stone bridge, advancing with the approach track to Whincop. Pass through the environs of this old steading – the name means 'gorse viewpoint'. Go left of the house down a short lane to a ladder-stile and flag bridge, keeping the wall to the left, amid bracken. Ignore the next ladder-stile, defended by a damp patch of ground, instead skirt right intent on the prominent rising scarp ridge. Ford the tiny gill and make up the rock spine with an evident path. The immediate views into Eskdale are quite lovely and warrant frequent contemplative pauses; the back drop of Scafell and the fell surround at the head of Eskdale are equally inspiring; the ridge culminates at the cairned top of Hartley Crag. Continue, dipping to cross the broken wall short of Gate Crag, the next transverse rise in the ridge. There is no straightforward route, a cairn again marks the top of this higher crest and again there is much for the eyes and camera. The natural route to the head of Birker Force is devoid of a path, but the terrain, though damp, is simple enough due east.

5 Pinch me and I'll admit my favourite route to the top begins from the Birkerfell Road, where the Devoke Water access track departs west. Go east, down the open road to High Ground. Bear right, with the wall left, upon the gated track signposted to Birkerthwaite. At the white-walled Ganny House Cottage branch off right to the gate in the paddock corner. Pass through the sheep pen, now with a wall left. Ignore the wall-stile by the next gate, glance on by rising gently to a broken stile/gate at the fence top. A grass path slants on below Great Crag towards the modest saddle. Where the remains of an old wall abuts the crag one may sportingly scramble up a steep ramp, or skirt round the crag altogether, mounting from the east: there are two cairned tops, excellent viewpoints. Hereon there is no path across rough fell in a northeasterly direction bound for the saddle north of the Green Crag stack. A ramp, high on the north side, giving access to the summit.   Return via Great Worm Crag.

Green Crag from the track to Birkerthwaite

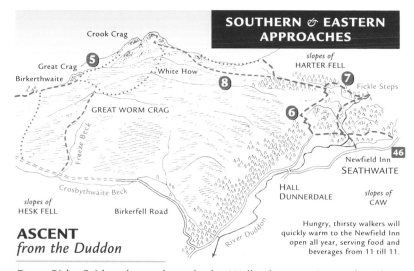

SOUTHERN & EASTERN APPROACHES

Crook Crag

Great Crag

Birkerthwaite

White How

slopes of HARTER FELL

Fickle Steps

GREAT WORM CRAG

Freeze Beck

Crosbythwaite Beck

slopes of HESK FELL

Birkerfell Road

Newfield Inn

SEATHWAITE

HALL DUNNERDALE

slopes of CAW

River Duddon

Hungry, thirsty walkers will quickly warm to the Newfield Inn open all year, serving food and beverages from 11 till 11.

ASCENT
from the Duddon

From Birks Bridge down through the Wallowbarrow Gorge the River Duddon is at its most impressive for walkers. The circuit from Newfield Inn up the gorge from the memorial footbridge to Fickle Steps, rising to Grassguards, turning back south on the track to High Wallowbarrow, is one of Lakeland's most cherished dale walks. If the fells are obliterated in mist and itchy feet can't be resisted then do this three-miler; naturally it's far better in sunshine. **6** Two paths converge on the memorial footbridge. One begins opposite the Newfield Inn, while the second begins at the School House, both cross Tarn Beck footbridges. Follow the path ahead into pasture, via gates, to reach High Wallowbarrow Farm. Turn right before the house, climbing via gates up to the saddle beside Wallowbarrow Crag, a popular venue for climbers – being low and south-facing the rock climbs are usually dry and quickly reached. An open track pursues a northerly course via deer-excluding double gates in the tall fence, entering a walled lane; note its massive drystone construction. The views hereabouts are quite delightful. Approaching Grassguards, take advantage of the permissive path avoiding the farmyard, skirt around the garden hedge, via hand-gates to reach Grassguard Gill. **7** This point can also be reached on a footpath ascending the gill from Fickle Steps. The stepping stones are fickle indeed; other than in drought conditions they are difficult to cross, despite the metal cable. The better approach is up the gorge from the memorial footbridge; the large boulder scree is a startling feature and the river tightly hemmed in with trees. **8** From Grassguards the path is clearly marked by gates and planks. Watch for the left turn at the top, as the footpath to Eskdale veers through the broken wall right. Cross a ladder-stile over the wall onto the open fell, a narrow trod pursuing a rather serpentine course WSW towards Green Crag. The summit is attained by rounding an outcrop, right then left.

CAW
STICKLE PIKE

White How, en route to Great Worm Crag

The Summit

The greatest crags face the west, the warming effect giving rise to the fell-name. The summit is ringed by rock walls which can be efficiently penetrated from two directions, via a ramp from the north and a small step from the east. Being a fell-top frequented by the more discerning walker the small summit cairn is not one prey to disturbance and looks old. The views are long, the string of tops to Black Combe outshone by the major summits of the Western and Mid-Western groups with the Coniston fells right of the nearby peaked summit of Harter Fell.

Safe Descents

Care is needed right from the start, particularly in mist. Backtrack by whichever of the two routes you arrived by, retracing familiar ground. Then aim north down to the broad grassy saddle. For reassurance find the embedded stone boundary marker in the midst of the saddle and take a bearing NE, crossing the featureless peaty tussocky moor. Cross a fence stile at the corner of forestry and join the Eskdale/Duddon path.

Ridge Routes to....

GREAT WORM CRAG   DESCENT 302*ft*   ASCENT 135*ft*   1.5 miles

An intermittent path holds to the broad ridge, some marsh to skirt, one nice top to stand upon, White How, at which point the ridge changes orientation from SSE to SW.

HARTER FELL   DESCENT 472*ft*   ASCENT 1,011*ft*   1.9 miles

Head down to the broad saddle N of the summit. Locate the boundary stone, take a bearing NE across the moor. Cross the fence stile at the NW end of the largely felled forestry. A clear path climbs, initially with the tall fence right, continuing ENE to the summit.

Green Crag from Crook Crag

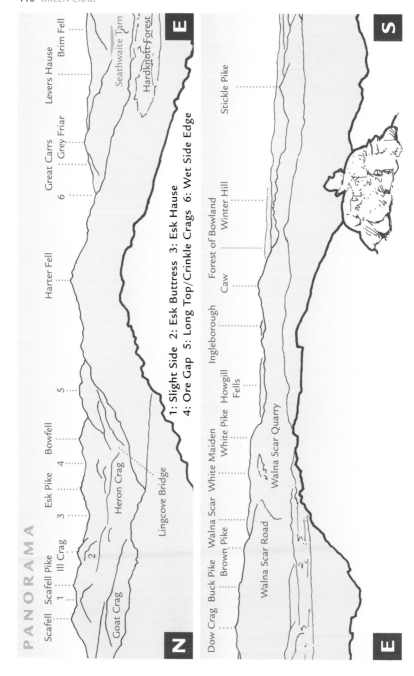

PANORAMA

Scafell Scafell Pike Esk Pike Bowfell Harter Fell Great Carrs Grey Friar Levers Hause Brim Fell

III Crag

1   2   3   4   5   6

Goat Crag Heron Crag Lingcove Bridge Seathwaite Tarn Hardknott Forest

N

E

1: Slight Side 2: Esk Buttress 3: Esk Hause
4: Ore Gap 5: Long Top/Crinkle Crags 6: Wet Side Edge

Dow Crag Buck Pike Walna Scar White Maiden White Pike Howgill Fells Ingleborough Forest of Bowland Caw Winter Hill Stickle Pike

Brown Pike

Walna Scar Road Walna Scar Quarry

E

S

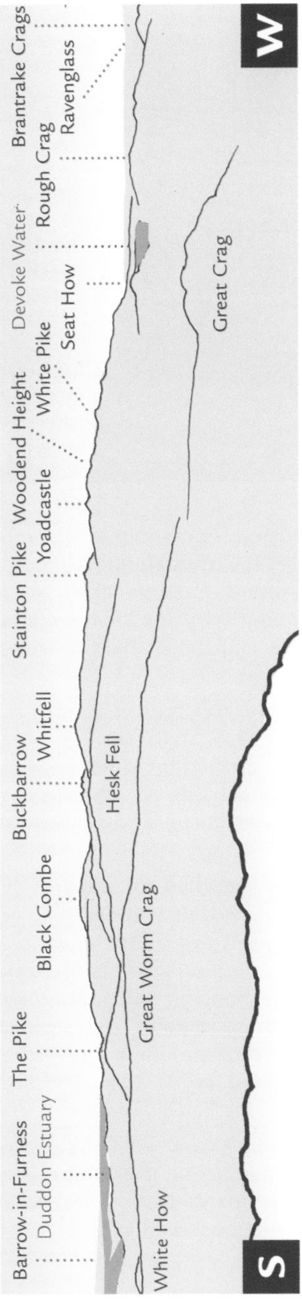

W (panel)

Brantrake Crags
Ravenglass
Rough Crag
Devoke Water
Seat How
White Pike
Woodend Height
Yoadcastle
Stainton Pike
Whitfell
Buckbarrow
Black Combe
The Pike
Barrow-in-Furness
Duddon Estuary

Great Crag
Hesk Fell
Great Worm Crag
White How

S (panel)

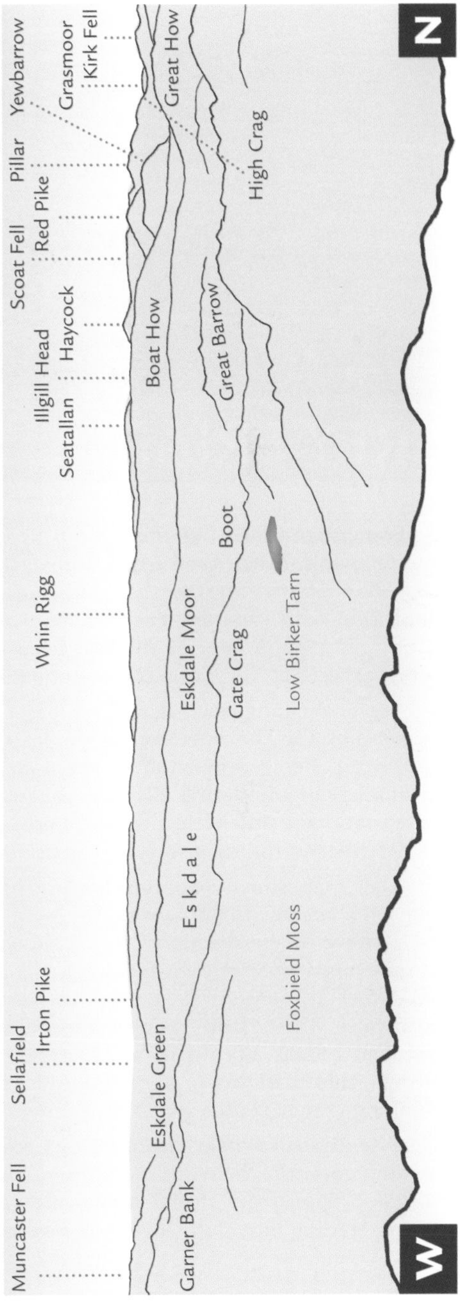

N (panel)

Yewbarrow
Grasmoor
Kirk Fell
Great How
High Crag
Pillar
Scoat Fell
Red Pike
Haycock
Illgill Head
Seatallan
Whin Rigg
Sellafield
Irton Pike
Muncaster Fell
Garner Bank

Boat How
Great Barrow
Eskdale Moor
Boot
Gate Crag
Low Birker Tarn
Eskdale
Eskdale Green
Foxbield Moss

W (panel)

The Franciscan friars, like the famous north Lakes huntsman John Peel, were renown for their grey attire, and so is this fell, though it is no more grey than many another. Perhaps the name has an early folk connection with itinerant Franciscans. Contemporary motor travellers do not get a good view of the fell. Even from Hardknott Pass it looks bulky, featureless and none too inviting.

Whatever the long view, as a climb it is a pleasurable bag, especially as a viewpoint for the northern outlook, with the Scafells seen in true proportion. Being tangential to the main Coniston ridge does restrict the number of wandering visitors. This may be considered a bonus for those that make the modest effort of crossing the Fairfield hause to rest beside either of the twin summit cairns.

The fell map shows just how nature has bequeathed an apparently dour fell a curious long low-rigg toe-hold in the verdancy of Seathwaite and a share in the drama of the Wallowbarrow Gorge. Of the water-courses most closely identified with the fell, the course of Tarn Beck needs special mention as it tumbles from the hanging valley cradling Seathwaite Tarn, leaping and bounding in excitement over great boulders. Seathwaite Tarn, an austere reservoir, may lack the more obvious charm of many a comparable Lakeland corrie tarn, yet the bounding craggy slopes give it a wild dignity.

Despite extensive rocky ground only Great and Little Blake Crags have climbing potential; beneath the former, a little further up the combe, are ruins and spoil from three small-scale copper mine levels. The head-stream, leading into Calf Cove, has several easily observed falls.

772 *metres*   2,533 *feet*

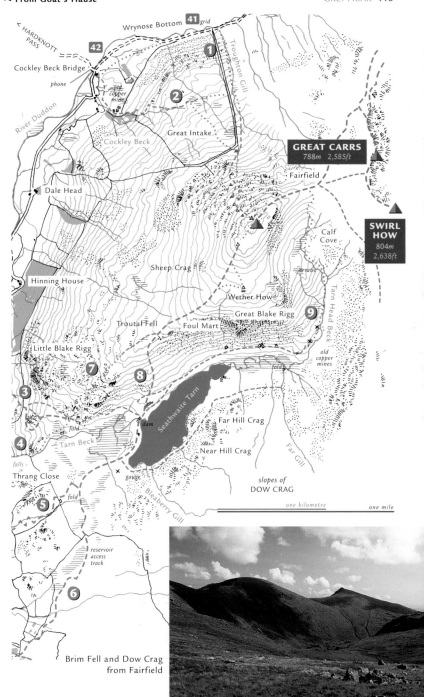

Wrynose Bottom 41 *grid*

< HARDKNOTT PASS

42

Cockley Beck Bridge

phone

old copper mine

1

2

River Duddon

Cockley Beck

Great Intake

GREAT CARRS
788m 2,585ft

Fairfield

SWIRL HOW
804m
2,638ft

Dale Head

Calf Cove

Troughton Gill

erratic

Sheep Crag

Hinning House

Wether How

Great Blake Rigg 9

Troutal Fell

Foul Mart

Tarn Head Beck

Little Blake Rigg

old copper mines

7

8

fold

3

Seathwaite Tarn

Far Hill Crag

fold

Tarn Beck

dam

4

Near Hill Crag

Far Gill

falls

Thrang Close

gauge

slopes of
DOW CRAG

fold

5

one kilometre   *one mile*

reservoir access track

Blesberry Gill

6

Brim Fell and Dow Crag
from Fairfield

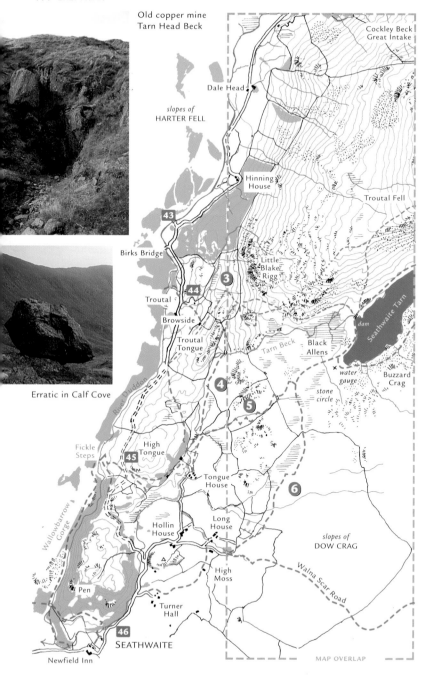

Old copper mine
Tarn Head Beck

Cockley Beck
Great Intake

Dale Head

slopes of
HARTER FELL

Hinning
House

Troutal Fell

43

Birks Bridge

Little
Blake
Rigg

3

Seathwaite Tarn

44

Troutal

dam

Browside

Troutal
Tongue

Tarn Beck

Black
Allens

× *water
gauge*

Buzzard
Crag

4

*stone
circle*

5

Erratic in Calf Cove

River Duddon

Fickle
Steps

High
Tongue

45

Tongue
House

6

Hollin
House

Long
House

slopes of
DOW CRAG

High
Moss

Walna Scar Road

Wallowbarrow Gorge

Pen

Turner
Hall

46

SEATHWAITE

Newfield Inn

MAP OVERLAP

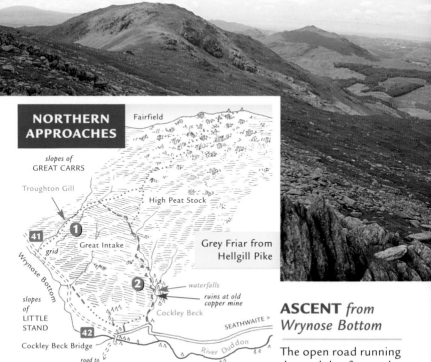

NORTHERN APPROACHES

Fairfield

slopes of
GREAT CARRS

Troughton Gill

High Peat Stock

41

1

grid

Great Intake

Grey Friar from
Hellgill Pike

2

waterfalls

ruins at old
copper mine

slopes
of
LITTLE
STAND

Cockley Beck

SEATHWAITE >

42

Cockley Beck Bridge

River Duddon

road to
HARDKNOTT PASS

Wrynose Bottom

ASCENT *from Wrynose Bottom*

The open road running down-dale from the Wrynose Pass crosses a cattle-grid at GR 257019. **1** Immediately before this a direct ascent of Grey Friar may begin. Climb the initially steep grass and boulder slope between Troughton Beck and the fence (no path). Rise to the top of the fenced (broken wall) enclosure. **2** This point may also be reached from Cockley Beck Bridge, where there is better casual car parking available and cottage tea-room. Immediately south of the house, find a stile guiding a footpath along the edge of a paddock to a wall-stile. Go right, over damp ground to join a track emerging behind the farm buildings. Follow this, winding uphill, pass the remains of an old copper mine *(right)* to a stile/gate. The track ventures onto the broad marshy shoulder. Bear SW, rising to a stile in the fence to meet the direct ascent. Go round to the left of the outcrop, with small cairns as guidance, climb quite steeply on a southerly course, dodging intermittent outcrops to reach the north top on the skyline.

LITTLE STAND

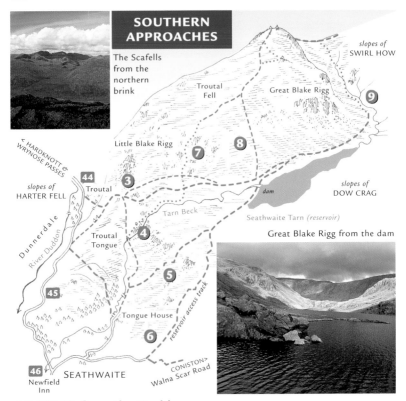

SOUTHERN APPROACHES

The Scafells from the northern brink

slopes of SWIRL HOW

Troutal Fell

Great Blake Rigg

HARDKNOTT & WRYNOSE PASSES

Little Blake Rigg

slopes of HARTER FELL

Troutal

Dunnerdale

River Duddon

Troutal Tongue

Tarn Beck

dam

slopes of DOW CRAG

Seathwaite Tarn (reservoir)

Great Blake Rigg from the dam

reservoir access track

Tongue House

CONISTON>
Walna Scar Road

Newfield Inn

SEATHWAITE

ASCENT *from the Duddon*

Lower down the valley a cluster of attractive approach routes begin, with Seathwaite Tarn dam the principal mid-point objective. **3** An efficient path starts from Troutal, following the gated approach track to Browside. Go left from the gate near the isolated house on a track through a further gate, soon switching uphill to a gateway in the top wall. Three paths could be followed from this point, but the best, a nice turf trod, is signposted right. This curves round an outcrop; coming up leftward watch for waymark posts guiding round marshy ground heading on towards the dam. **4** A superb second option homing in on this tract of fell explores the delights of the Tarn Beck valley from Seathwaite, a road walk via Hollin House to Tongue House; or you can park on the common above Fickle Steps GR 231974 and trace the footpath east down through bracken and woodland behind a barn into pasture at a stile; either continue to Tongue House, or go left by Thrang Cottage and on to a hand-gate and cross small footbridge over Tarn Beck. A footpath now accompanies the beck upstream, avoiding wet ground as best it can,

Tarn Beck... *the rain that falls on the fells, flees from the fells down falls*

heading for a wooden footbridge at the bottom of the Tarn Beck cascades. While walkers will be grateful for the standard issue footbridge, many may consider the setting deserved a more 'beautilitarian' model. The footpath continues via a ladder-stile and gate to link up with the previously described route, with an option to visit the actual top of Troutal Tongue, left, over a stile at the ridge-end, a superb viewpoint for Harter Fell *(see page 124)*. DEFINITION: Troutal = *trout-hall,* Tongue = *a low jutting gesturing ridge.* But the really exciting choice branches off up the rough north bank, through the bracken, climbing through the breach where the wall meets the falls, scrambling easily up the sequence of great boulder steps beside the amazing fuming falls. Once upon the level wet moor, go left from the old sheepfold to the contouring path, or **7** climb straight on up the fellside, aiming for the notch in the skyline onto Troutal Fell, by a narrow path discerned once on the ridge. **5** A well-used footpath also winds up the rough pastures from Tongue House to meet the reservoir access track. **6** For greatest ease, follow the Walna Scar Road up from Seathwaite; as it turns to a track at a gate, take the left branch via a further gate, this being the free-running access track to the dam. Cross the dam wall footway. **8** From this point a direct ascent heads straight ahead up the obvious rigg slightly east of north onto Troutal Fell, a clear path underfoot. This is a very pleasant approach; an at-a-whim deviation right can bring in the cairn on the prominent pike of Wether How, high above Great Blake Rigg. The summit dome seems quite distant for much of the way until the ultimate plateau is reached at a guide cairn. **9** The path that leads along the northern shore of Seathwaite Tarn is rather more likely to be used as a return leg, but venturing into the headstream via Calf Cove is a genuinely interesting expedition. Beyond the reservoir the path passes an area of copper mining activity via a spoil apron, a good pitch for a wild camp. Passing ruined miners' dens vacated in the early nineteenth century, a dwindling path contours by two further blocked mine levels with associated spoil tongues and ruined stone huts. Follow the eastern bank of Tarn Head Beck climbing steadily into Calf Cove, passing successive specimens of perched erratics, fine subjects for the camera, climbing pathless to the skyline of Fairfield. Go left (west), now with the clear ridge path.

The Summit

A gentle dome informally interspersed with low outcropping, two parallel ribs, some 36 metres apart, each surmounted by a cairn, define the highest ground. The summit looks south to the less flattering aspect of Brim Fell, Coniston Old Man and Dow Crag, while to the north it commands a peach of a view *(see page 112)*. Man-watching fell-top visitors is an interesting pastime in itself – perhaps deserving a thesis – as so often walkers casually miss the best prospects by assuming the summit is *the* place to halt. Having visited this spot three times this season, the author has seen walkers ignore the northern cairn on each occasion.

North top *(left)* and the summit

Safe Descents

In mist a plateau top like this can be troublesome, remembering that craggy slopes are tucked under the broad SE and NW edges, the SE the more treacherous. Cautious walkers can thread down through the broken northwestern slopes en route to Cockley Beck Bridge in low cloud. However, it is far better to take a bearing SW onto Troutal Fell, seeking the easier slopes leading to the Seathwaite Tarn dam. Though more long-winded, the slopes leading into Calf Cove from Fairfield hause are quite benign, walk ENE to the grassy col, then slip pathless into the hollow, keeping in harmony with Tarn Head Beck; avoid the valley marshes in traversing above Seathwaite Tarn. The two routes converge at the concrete dam; either follow the open path to the N of the outflowing beck to reach Troutal via Browside or, having crossed the dam, join the assured track to the metalled Walna Scar road leading to Seathwaite...

and an Inn!

Ridge Route to...

GREAT CARRS DESCENT 478 *ft*   ASCENT 423 *ft*   0.7 miles

If all ridge routes were this simple (guidance necessary in mist). From the summit cairn aim NE, pass the Matterhorn Rock *(below)*, descending with the ridge path, arrive upon a three-way fork on Fairfield hause. Take the middle course ENE, up the largely grassy slope to the summit.

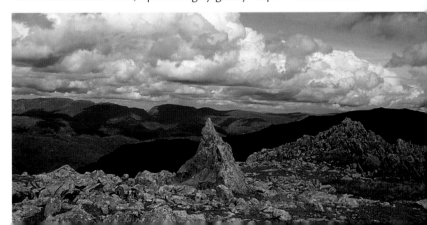

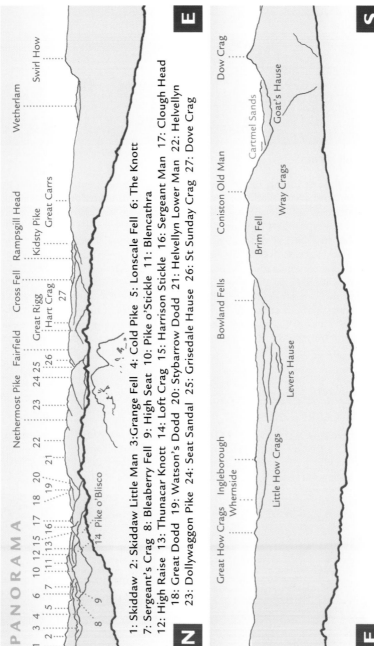

PANORAMA

E

S

N

E

Swirl How

Wetherlam

Rampsgill Head

Cross Fell

Nethermost Pike Fairfield

Great Carrs

Kidsty Pike

Great Rigg

Hart Crag

27

26

24 25

23

22

21

18 20

19

17 16 15 12 10 6 4 3 1

11 13 5 2

7

9

8

Pike o'Blisco

14

Dow Crag

Cartmel Sands

Goat's Hause

Coniston Old Man

Wray Crags

Bowland Fells

Brim Fell

Levers Hause

Great How Crags Ingleborough

Whernside

Little How Crags

1: Skiddaw 2: Skiddaw Little Man 3:Grange Fell 4: Cold Pike 5: Lonscale Fell 6: The Knott
7: Sergeant's Crag 8: Bleaberry Fell 9: High Seat 10: Pike o'Stickle 11: Blencathra
12: High Raise 13: Thunacar Knott 14: Loft Crag 15: Harrison Stickle 16: Sergeant Man 17: Clough Head
18: Great Dodd 19: Watson's Dodd 20: Stybarrow Dodd 21: Helvellyn Lower Man 22: Helvellyn
23: Dollywaggon Pike 24: Seat Sandal 25: Grisedale Hause 26: St Sunday Crag 27: Dove Crag

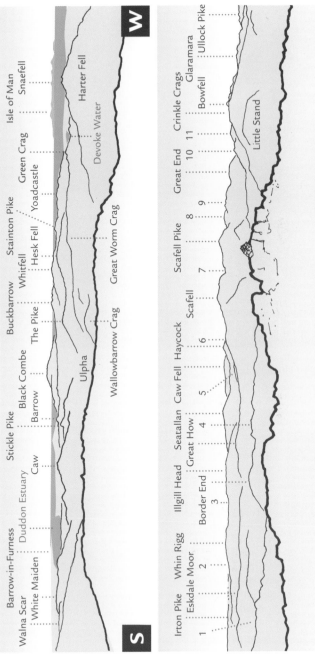

W

S

N

W

Isle of Man
Snaefell

Harter Fell

Devoke Water

Green Crag

Yoadcastle

Stainton Pike

Whitfell
Hesk Fell

Buckbarrow

The Pike

Great Worm Crag

Black Combe

Barrow

Ulpha

Wallowbarrow Crag

Stickle Pike

Caw

Duddon Estuary

Barrow-in-Furness

Walna Scar
White Maiden

Crinkle Crags

Glaramara

Great End
10 11

Bowfell

Ullock Pike

Little Stand

Scafell Pike

9

8

7

Scafell

Haycock
Caw Fell

6

Seatallan

5

Great How

Illgill Head
Whin Rigg

4

Border End

3

Irton Pike

Eskdale Moor

2

1

1: Boot 2: Sellafield 3: Ponsonby Fell 4: Hard Knott 5: Yewbarrow 6: Slight Side
7: Mickledore 8: Broad Crag 9: Ill Crag 10: Pike de Bield 11: Esk Pike

HARTER FELL   12

Every inch a fellwalker's fell, there are no climbs here, for all that rock abounds, especially on the summit. And what a summit... a playground for scramblers, and a viewpoint for dreamers. The fell rises to a crag-topped peak catching the travellers' eye, whether from the Duddon at

Cockley Beck Bridge or during the traverse of Hardknott Pass from where its heather-tiered craggy northern slopes are really well seen. Best of all, admire it from Eskdale where it rises from the woods and meadows to a sceptred peak. A fell of great individuality and no little beauty, marking the real beginning of the high fells from the southwest. By choice climb Harter from Eskdale and sense for yourself the wonderful setting. The conifers of Hardknott Forest that have of recent years dominated its lower southern and eastern slopes have come of age, and great swathes have been felled; plans are afoot to meld a far more diverse woodland patchwork to grace the Duddon dale.

The Duddon from Birks Bridge

653 *metres*   2,142 *feet*

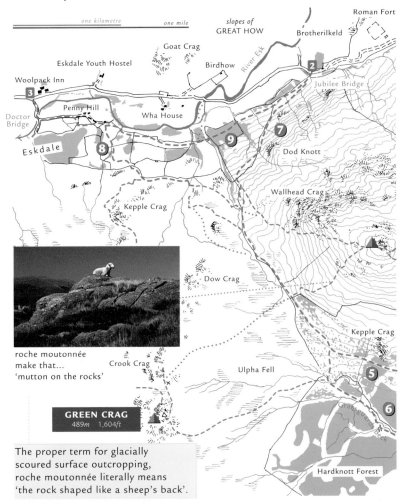

roche moutonnée
make that...
'mutton on the rocks'

GREEN CRAG
489m   1,604ft

The proper term for glacially
scoured surface outcropping,
roche moutonnée literally means
'the rock shaped like a sheep's back'.

ASCENT *from Hardknott Pass*

1 From the top of the pass cross the cattle-grid and descend with the
road on the west side to where a bridleway is signposted left. Follow this
path south, ignore the electric fence stile, glance to the right of the
broken wall corner, to cross a fence stile. The continuing path traverses
an undulating marshy tract of fell, with the upper fringe of forestry close
left; drift right to cross a further fence stile. A clear path climbs steadily
over heathery ground, pitching through a gully, headstream of Castlehow
Beck, rising to join the path from Birks Bridge as the summit tors are
met. Approach the summit from the east through a natural breach.

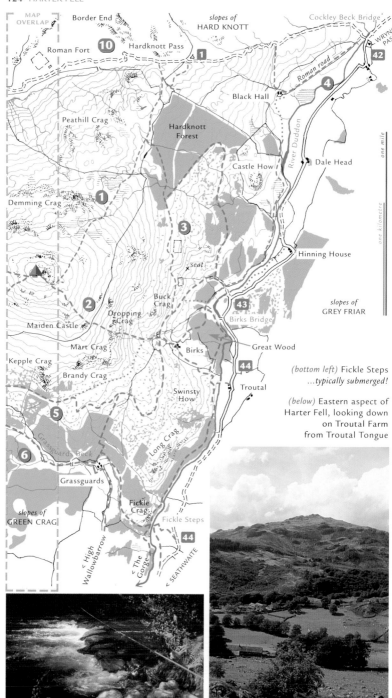

MAP OVERLAP

Border End

slopes of HARD KNOTT

Cockley Beck Bridge

Roman Fort

10 Hardknott Pass

△ **1**

WRYNOSE PASS >

42

Roman road

4

Black Hall

River Duddon

Peathill Crag

Hardknott Forest

one mile

Castle How

Dale Head

Demming Crag

1

3

seal

Hinning House

2

Dropping Crag

Buck Crag

Birks Bridge

43

slopes of GREY FRIAR

Maiden Castle

Mart Crag

Great Wood

Kepple Crag

Birks

44

Brandy Crag

Swinsty How

Troutal

5

one kilometre

Grassguards Beck

Long Crag

(bottom left) Fickle Steps
...typically submerged!

6

(below) Eastern aspect of
Harter Fell, looking down
on Troutal Farm
from Troutal Tongue

Grassguards

Fickle Crag

slopes of GREEN CRAG

Fickle Steps

High Wallowbarrow

The Gorge

44

< SEATHWAITE

Looking down on the Hard Knott Roman Fort backed by the mighty Scafells

ASCENT *from the Duddon*

2 From the picturesque environs of Birks Bridge follow a waymarked bridle-path up through the oaks of Great Wood and by the Shropshire outdoor centre at Birks onto a track leading to a transverse forest track, which may be followed more directly from the Birks Bridge car park. Seek the low waymark posts guiding a foot-path up by old walled enclosures in the forest, by a felled hollow up the steep bank due west, climbing beside the stony gill onto the heather banks leading to a fence stile.

Birks Bridge

Above this, pass an outcrop with the romantic name Maiden Castle; soon grass replaces the ling as the summit rock bluffs draw near. **3** A seldom trod footpath runs across the fellside almost due north from the forest track, crossing a further forest track, completing the climb through the 'Black Forest' of residual conifers to a hand-gate onto the open fell joining the path from Hardknott Pass.

Stepping steeply down through the purple heather between Dropping and Mart Crags

EASTERN APPROACHES

Demming Crag

Border End

Hardknott Pass

Birks

Hardknott Forest

Black Hall

River Duddon

45

Fickle Steps

44 Troutal

43

Birks Bridge

slopes of GREY FRIAR

42

4 It would be more than remiss not to mention the valley path from Cockley Beck Bridge which can be followed all the way down to High Wallowbarrow, a distance of four miles, most of the way close to the river. A journey of great contrasts, it begins on the farm track thought to lie upon the Roman road which switched up to Harknott from Black Hall – a former youth hostel, now a base for tetchy sheep dogs (the author got nipped for his pains). Traversing meadows the trail comes close to the river beneath Castle How, heading on by Birks Bridge, where woodland envelopes its passage and rocky bluffs cause it to rise and fall behind Troutal. Now enter a short dense forest passage to Fickle Steps, cross Grassguards Beck footbridge, and the grand finale approaches, climbing briefly to dip into the luxuriant confines of the Wallowbarrow Gorge, with its massive boulder scree – quite superb.

5 Forest tracks, either from Birks or Grassguards, converge to rise across the southern slopes of Harter Fell, focusing on the ancient pedestrian pass leading into lovely Eskdale.

6 This old trail emanates from Grassguards, which can be reached from Fickle Steps direct, or on the track from High Wallowbarrow, by either route an attractive walk. The path follows Grassguards Gill via a gate, then plank footbridge, with young conifers to left, mature specimens right, in an open tract, crossing through a broken wall right, as the Green Crag path branches left. Advance to exit the forest at a hand-gate in the fence. Here turn sharp right, climbing first with the tall fence, then on open fell on a good path to the top.

Retired potato-lifter at Penny Hill in upper Eskdale, with Harter Fell in the background

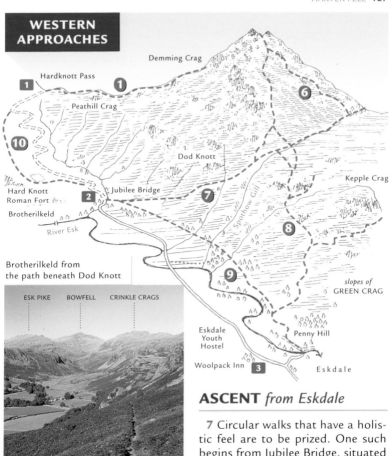

WESTERN APPROACHES

Demming Crag

Hardknott Pass

1 **1**

Peathill Crag

6

10

Dod Knott

Kepple Crag

Hard Knott
Roman Fort **2** Jubilee Bridge

Brotherilkeld **7**

River Esk Spothow Gill

8

Brotherilkeld from
the path beneath Dod Knott

slopes of
GREEN CRAG

9

ESK PIKE BOWFELL CRINKLE CRAGS

Eskdale
Youth
Hostel

Penny Hill

Woolpack Inn **3** Eskdale

ASCENT *from Eskdale*

7 Circular walks that have a holis-
tic feel are to be prized. One such
begins from Jubilee Bridge, situated
at the foot of the Hardknott Pass,
and combines the ascent of Harter
Fell with a visit to the Roman Fort
on the rigg overlooking the upper
Eskdale gorge **1&10**, with en route
scenic moments galore. Cross the
little stone footbridge built in 1977 to commemorate the silver jubilee of
the Queen's accession to the throne in 1952. Pass through successive
kissing-gates and be sure to take the peat road, the more obvious made
path, ahead. This green way duly begins to rise as might a mine incline.
The view back into upper Eskdale is a scene to savour *(see above)*, a grand
girdle of Lakeland's mightiest fells conclusively rim the horizon and in the
green dale farm names such as Wha House, Taw House and Brotherilkeld, reflect roots in the Scandinavian farming settlement of the area.

Climb on through the bracken via two hand-gates, with constant cause to stop and admire the view. The path from Boot merges from the right. Now bear away from the notoriously marshy path that runs on beside the moorland flanking fence, destination Grassguards; a clear ascending path takes precedence. Ascend with the occasional pitched steps to join forces with the path risen from the forest edge, beneath a classic volcanically contorted outcrop, advancing to the gap between the summit battlements.

8 From Boot either follow the Eskdale Trail to Doctor Bridge, or start from the Woolpack Inn following the road west to the lane signed 'Penny Hill', which leads over the said bridge, a lovely spot to look into the cool clear waters of the Esk. The river-name quite simply means 'source', a variant of Exe in Devon and Axe in Staffordshire. Go straight ahead along the hedged, then walled, lane towards Penny Hill Farm. A permissive path, via gates, ushers walkers right then left, avoiding the farmyard. Rejoin the track east of the farm, go through a gate and, as the track forks, go right, rising to a gate; the path veers up left, rising to a wall; glance right to a gate by old pens, continue up the turf peat road. At the right-hand bend see a wooden signpost with the legend 'Harter Fell' guiding left. The path traverses with the intake wall to the left and below, slipping through a re-entrant gill, aims diagonally up the facing slope and through a gap in the outcropping en route to a ford at Spothow Gill and stile in the fence there joining the path from Jubilee Bridge.

9 The Eskdale Trail crops up from time to time in this guide. A particularly choice passage leads down from Jubilee Bridge to Doctor Bridge, largely a meadow-way giving a pleasing end to a day's walk over Harter Fell. **10** A bridleway leads off the Hardknott Pass road at the top hairpin. This leads down past the Roman parade ground and along the scarp by the Roman Fort, to re-join the road just above Jubilee Bridge.

The summit outcrop from the east – figure with binoculars is looking into Eskdale

The Summit

The summit is unmistakable *(right)* but whether you choose to clamber onto it is another matter! The more modest situation of the Ordnance Survey column suffices for many visitors *(below)*. The view is the real bounty, a grand panorama with the Scafells and the head of Eskdale seen to perfection.

Safe Descents

First rule of thumb when leaving the summit of Harter Fell, if there is a path underfoot, you can be confident that it takes you to safety - E to Birks, W to Boot and N to the top of the Hardknott Pass.

Ridge Route to...

GREEN CRAG   DESCENT 1,011*ft*
ASCENT 472*ft*   1.9 miles

Follow the regular path descending WSW, watching to take the left fork below the intensely contorted volcanic outcrop; this path leads down to the edge of the forestry. Glance by the tall fence, ignoring the 'Pass' path crossing the fence stile in the corner. Take a bearing SW across the rough peaty moor to enter the broad grassy saddle between Crook and Green Crags. Climb the bank S to gain the summit from the E.

The summit outcrop from the lower southern rock bastion

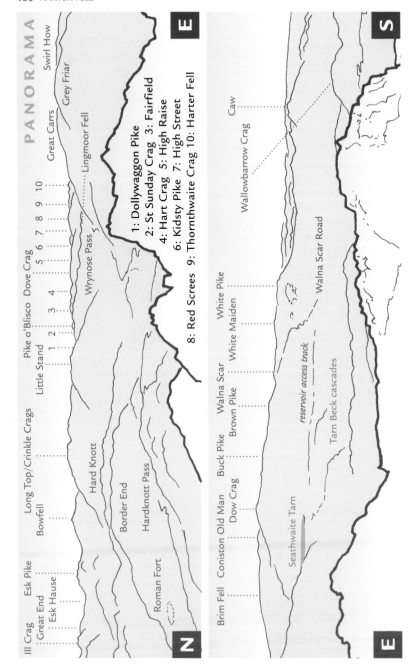

PANORAMA

E

Swirl How
Grey Friar
Great Carrs
Lingmoor Fell

1: Dollywaggon Pike
2: St Sunday Crag 3: Fairfield
4: Hart Crag 5: High Raise
6: Kidsty Pike 7: High Street
8: Red Screes 9: Thornthwaite Crag 10: Harter Fell

Pike o'Blisco Dove Crag
Little Stand

5 6 7 8 9 10
1 2 3 4

Wrynose Pass

Long Top/Crinkle Crags
Bowfell

Hard Knott

Border End

Hardknott Pass

Esk Pike
Great End
Esk Hause
Ill Crag

Roman Fort

N

S

Caw
Wallowbarrow Crag

White Pike
White Maiden

Walna Scar Road

Walna Scar
Brown Pike

Buck Pike

reservoir access track

Tarn Beck cascades

Brim Fell Coniston Old Man
Dow Crag

Seathwaite Tarn

E

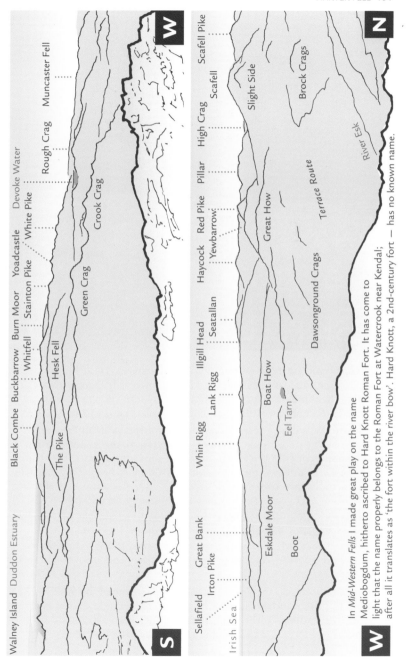

N

Scafell Pike

Scafell

Slight Side

Brock Crags

High Crag

Pillar

Red Pike

Haycock

River Esk

Terrace Route

Great How

Yewbarrow

Seatallan

Illgill Head

Dawsonground Crags

Lank Rigg

Boat How

Whin Rigg

Eel Tarn

Eskdale Moor

Boot

Great Bank

Irton Pike

Sellafield

Irish Sea

W

W

Muncaster Fell

Rough Crag

Devoke Water

White Pike

Yoadcastle

Crook Crag

Stainton Pike

Burn Moor

Whitfell

Buckbarrow

Green Crag

Black Combe

Hesk Fell

The Pike

Duddon Estuary

Walney Island

S

In *Mid-Western Fells* I made great play on the name Mediobogdum, hitherto ascribed to Hard Knott Roman Fort. It has come to light that the name properly belongs to the Roman Fort at Watercrook near Kendal; after all it translates as 'the fort within the river bow'. Hard Knott, a 2nd-century fort — has no known name.

HESK FELL

Let's not be too hasty, even puddings can be sweet. Hesk Fell may look like a Pennine outcast but it has interesting historic features to seek out, including the remains of a copper mine and a large Viking enclosure, and with the Pike, makes a striking connection with the Duddon.

Rainsborrow Wood, presently undergoing a radical transformation to reinvigorate its deciduous diversity, hangs from the eastern scarp of The Pike, and enriches the look and feel of the Duddon vale from Ulpha. Pike Side Farm add to the scene with its Organic Farm Trail, drawing attention to its rare sweet meadows unsullied by fertiliser and chemical treatments – this year's cut hay smelt sublime, good enough to eat!

The farms along its Duddon base provide resource for Original Cumbrian Wool: a dynamic local venture turning the otherwise largely worthless fleece of Herdwick, and other traditional upland sheep breeds, into coveted, naturally undyed fabric products, much softer than you'd expect.

The main body of the fell is presently partitioned by electric heaf fencing, but the wanderer is suitably acknowledged and accommodated with strategic stiles. To the west of the fell lies the vast upland bowl of Storthes, a wilderness wherein even sheep may look lonely.

476 *metres*   1,562 *feet*

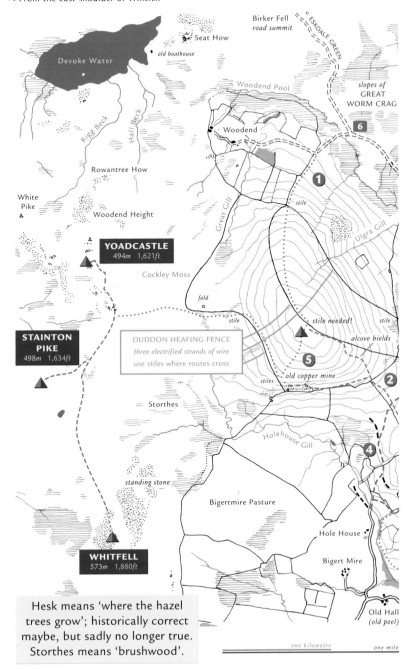

Birker Fell
road summit

ESKDALE GREEN

Seat How

old boathouse

Woodend Pool

slopes of
GREAT
WORM CRAG

Devoke Water

Woodend

6

1

stile

Ulgra Gill

Rigg Beck

Hall Beck

Rowantree How

White
Pike
△

Woodend Height

Great Gill

YOADCASTLE
494m   1,621ft

Cockley Moss

fold

stile

stile needed!

stile

alcove bields

**STAINTON
PIKE**
498m   1,634ft

DUDDON HEAFING FENCE
*three electrified strands of wire
use stiles where routes cross*

5

old copper mine

2

stiles

Storthes

standing stone

Holehouse Gill

4

Bigertmire Pasture

Hole House

Bigert Mire

WHITFELL
573m   1,880ft

Old Hall
(old peel)

Hesk means 'where the hazel
trees grow'; historically correct
maybe, but sadly no longer true.
Storthes means 'brushwood'.

one kilometre   one mile

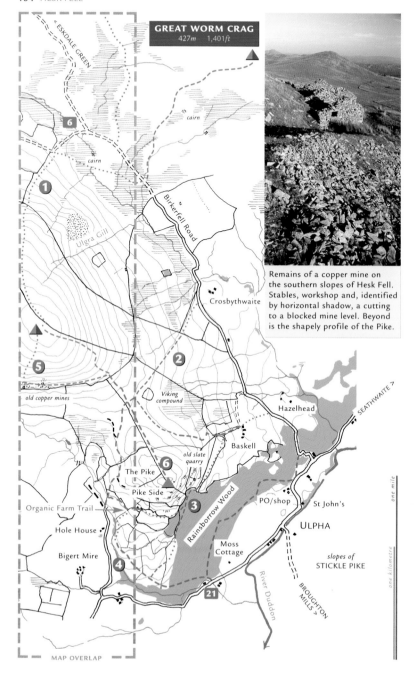

GREAT WORM CRAG
427m   1,401ft

ESKDALE GREEN

cairn

6

1

cairn

Birkerfell Road

Ulgra Gill

Crosbythwaite

2

5

old copper mines

Viking compound

Hazelhead

SEATHWAITE >

Baskell

old slate quarry

The Pike

6

Pike Side

Organic Farm Trail

3

Rainsborrow Wood

PO/shop   St John's

ULPHA

Hole House

Bigert Mire

Moss Cottage

slopes of STICKLE PIKE

4

21

River Duddon

BROUGHTON MILLS >

one mile

one kilometre

MAP OVERLAP

Remains of a copper mine on the southern slopes of Hesk Fell. Stables, workshop and, identified by horizontal shadow, a cutting to a blocked mine level. Beyond is the shapely profile of the Pike.

ASCENT *from Woodend Bridge & Bobbinmill Bridge*

1 Woodend Bridge GR 328047 off the Birkerfell Road is a common start point, for all it lacks an obvious imaginative return. Walk to the gate, entry into the walled enclosures leading to Woodend Farm; ignore this, follow up the pasture left, keeping the wall to the right until confronted by the electric heaf fencing, cross the stile. Ascend the featureless ridge, coming alongside a second fence traversing the fell-top. Well not quite, for a few stones have been jealously gathered to form a summit cairn on the south side, necessitating a nifty step-over. **2** A bridleway leaves the Birkerfell Road east of the entrance to Crosbythwaite Farm, by a series of gates reaches the ridge wall *(see above)*, passing close to the remnants of a D-shaped Viking stock enclosure, in excess of an acre in size – it's a rare survival. To revel in the special view from the Pike **6** accessible left, keep the ridge wall close right, via a stile. Heed the notice on the summit; it's not worth even thinking about an eastward descent. For Hesk Fell leave the bridleway right, following the wall up to a ladder-stile, climb the facing slope: note several small stone alcoves higher up, created as modest bield shelters, replicating the scrapes sheep naturally fashion themselves for the purpose. **3** From Bobbinmill Bridge footpaths climb through the Rainsborrow Wood via kissing-gates and ladder-stiles on a permissive path at Pike Side Farm to gain the ridge coincident with the bridleway from Crosbythwaite. The footpath through the top of Rainsborrow is a special treat, leading into a narrow lateral enclosure, then to an old mine path climbing from Baskell Farm via gates. **5** An interesting variant path, a miners' trod, contours from the ladder-stile GR 182943 to inspect enigmatic remains of the early nineteenth-century copper mine. Climb up the open fellside north to gain the summit. See the map on page 141 for ridge route connections with:

Yoadcastle 1.4 miles and Stainton Pike 1.6 miles

PANORAMA

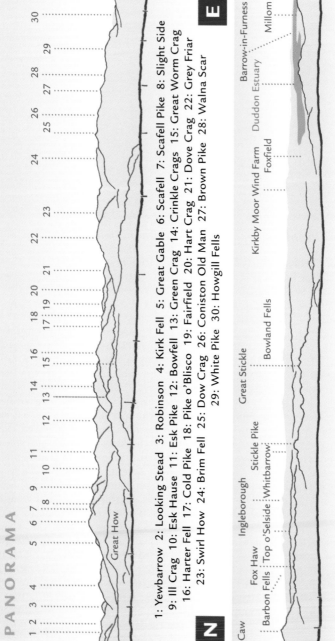

1: Yewbarrow 2: Looking Stead 3: Robinson 4: Kirk Fell 5: Great Gable 6: Scafell 7: Scafell Pike 8: Slight Side
9: Ill Crag 10: Esk Hause 11: Esk Pike 12: Bowfell 13: Green Crag 14: Crinkle Crags 15: Great Worm Crag
16: Harter Fell 17: Cold Pike 18: Pike o'Blisco 19: Fairfield 20: Hart Crag 21: Dove Crag 22: Grey Friar
23: Swirl How 24: Brim Fell 25: Dow Crag 26: Coniston Old Man 27: Brown Pike 28: Walna Scar
29: White Pike 30: Howgill Fells

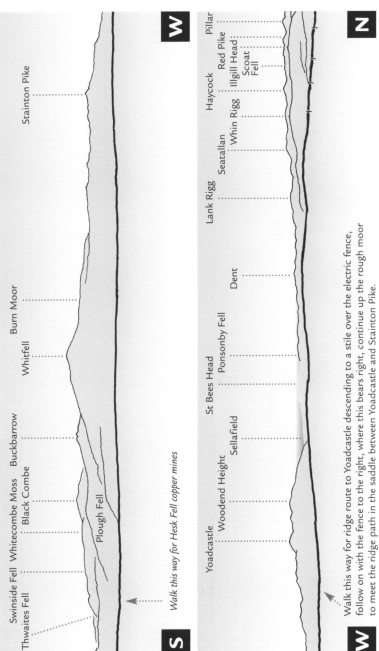

W

Stainton Pike

Thwaites Fell
Swinside Fell
Whitecombe Moss
Black Combe
Buckbarrow
Whitfell
Burn Moor

Plough Fell

Walk this way for Hesk Fell copper mines

S

N

Lank Rigg
Seatallan
Whin Rigg
Haycock
Illgill Head
Scoat Fell
Red Pike
Pillar

Dent

Yoadcastle
Woodend Height
Sellafield
St Bees Head
Ponsonby Fell

W

Walk this way for ridge route to Yoadcastle descending to a stile over the electric fence, follow on with the fence to the right, where this bears right, continue up the rough moor to meet the ridge path in the saddle between Yoadcastle and Stainton Pike.

PANORAMA from the Pike

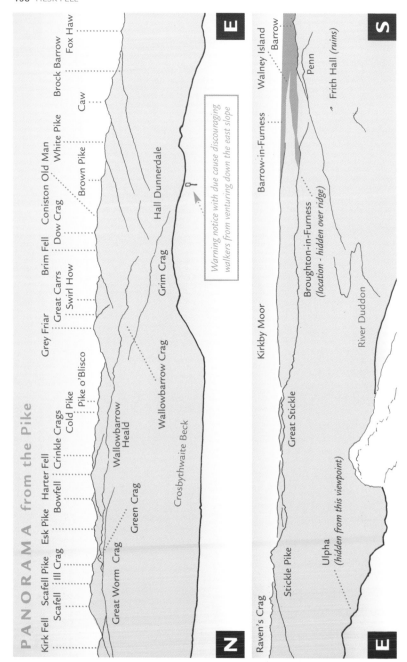

Warning notice with due cause discouraging walkers from venturing down the east slope

Top panorama (N / E):

Kirk Fell — Scafell — Scafell Pike — Ill Crag — Esk Pike — Bowfell — Harter Fell — Crinkle Crags — Cold Pike — Pike o'Blisco — Grey Friar — Great Carrs — Swirl How — Brim Fell — Coniston Old Man — Dow Crag — White Pike — Brown Pike — Caw — Brock Barrow — Fox Haw

Great Worm Crag — Green Crag — Wallowbarrow Heald — Wallowbarrow Crag — Grim Crag — Hall Dunnerdale — Crosbythwaite Beck

Bottom panorama (E / S):

Raven's Crag — Stickle Pike — Ulpha (hidden from this viewpoint) — Great Stickle — Kirkby Moor — Broughton-in-Furness (location - hidden over ridge) — Barrow-in-Furness — Walney Island — Barrow — Penn — Frith Hall (ruins) — River Duddon

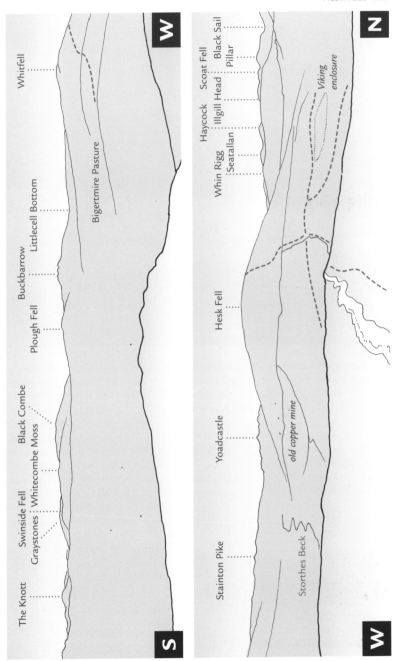

Top panel (W to S):

The Knott — Graystones · Swinside Fell — Whitecombe Moss — Black Combe — Plough Fell — Buckbarrow — Littlecell Bottom — Whitfell

Bigertmire Pasture

Bottom panel (N to W):

Stainton Pike — Yoadcastle — Hesk Fell — Whin Rigg · Seatallan — Haycock · Illgill Head — Scoat Fell · Black Sail — Pillar

Storthes Beck — old copper mine — Viking enclosure

HOLME FELL   14

Growing due south from the hamlet of Little Langdale, a southerly rising wooded ridge that comes of age above Yewdale's lovely parkland. One of the great little fells of Lakeland, Holme Fell's southernmost facade of rocky ribs jut through a dense cover of native trees *(above)*, giving it an air of impregnability. Within its woods and upland pastures lurks a diverse wildlife. Of special note, before the bracken runs riot, are swathes of bluebells mingling with the birch. The dust and noise of slate quarrying has largely died away but its effects remain. Nature has done a fine cover-up job to create a place of sylvan peace where once man toiled. The fell offers far more than a good ridge walk. Circular strolls abound investigating wooded glens around the compass, with Tilberthwaite and the extraordinary quarried hollows at Hodge Close, fascinating places to discover.

The larger of a pair of dams NW of Uskdale Gap: a miniature Tarn Hows. Helvellyn and Fairfield form the mountain backdrop.

317 *metres*   1,040 *feet*

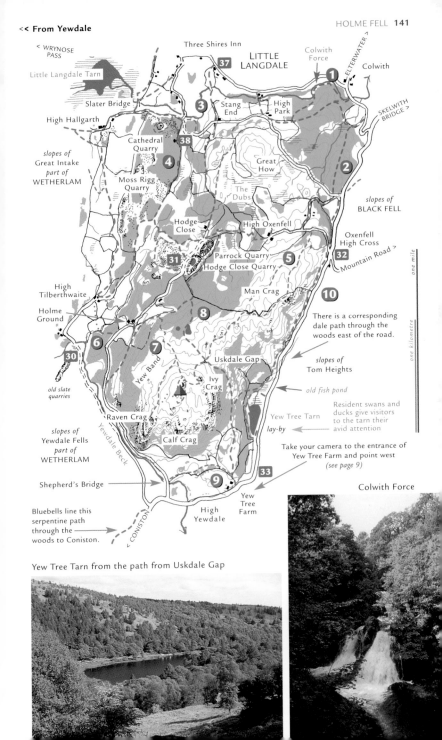

Yew Tree Tarn from the path from Uskdale Gap

Colwith Force

ASCENT *from Little Langdale*

Hiding behind a mantle of trees, Holme Fell is largely obscured from the Little Langdale valley, but from a choice of four routes one may begin to unravel its secrets. **1** The Cumbria Way climbs out of the Colwith woods, and having inspected the thunderous force, emerges via hand-gates at High Park. Follow the road west to a footpath signed left, short of Stang End. This leads via a stile across the wet marsh of Little Fell, close by Great How to enter woodland at a gate joining the Stang End /Hodge Close track. **2** Another woodland path, missing the falls, heads up due south to join the High Park road at its junction with the Coniston road; follow either a fenced roadside path leading to High Cross, or a quiet byroad leading direct to High Oxenfell Farm.

3 From the community of Little Langdale a footpath leaves the road at a kissing-gate 275 metres east of Wilson Place at GR 318033. Descending the pasture, cross a footbridge, a lovely spot to enjoy the sparkling beck before advancing into a lane leading to Stang End. **4** From Three Shires Inn go 90 metres west to the minor road junction, take the descending lane winding down by several handsomely sited houses to the ford and raised footbridge. Continue south along the track leading through a valley glade ultimate destination High Tilberthwaite Farm. After the high spoil of Moss Rigg quarry watch for the leftward branching track in woodland, leading to the small community of Hodge Close.

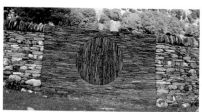

Andy Goldsworthy brings out the beauty of slate within its native setting with this stylised sheepfold at Low Tilberthwaite.

The sheer raw grandeur of slate where Parrock and Hodge Close quarries connect

5 From Oxenfell High Cross one may cheerfully follow the road to, and through, High Oxenfell Farm and pursue the subsequent gated track to Hodge Close – a useful connection when making a round walk orbiting the entire fell. But the prime attention must go to getting onto the Holme Fell ridge proper and this is easily achieved at the top of the first rise in this by road, where a recessed gate left gives access onto the fell by power-lines. A definite path passes a pool onto the emerging ridge: young deciduous tree plantings confirm that the landscape is pro-actively managed by the National Trust; the grazing is also moderated to suit regeneration of the native habitat. The path mounts a prominent knoll, then follows a metal fence, in season past an area of bluebells; note an old cairn prominent well to the west of the ridge path. The path crosses a stile as the fence straddles the ridge and descends amongst the rank heather. As the fence bears right, ignore the carpet-wrapped stile, keep left to thread through rocky knots and by a solitary larch on an undulating path to arrive at the Uskdale Gap cairn *(see above)*. Ivy Crag rises ahead, surmounted by the fell's largest cairn. Climb direct to this prominent shoulder, a very good viewpoint for Tom Heights and Black Fell. The summit is attained by skirting right, by a marsh, with a worn path stepping up the right-hand edge.

Holme Fell from the Mountain Road

ASCENT *from Yewdale*

The saddle of Uskdale Gap is the focus of all but one ascents accessed from the footpath which crosses the ridge from east to west. **6** From Low Tilberthwaite follow the road almost to High Tilberthwaite, take the gated footpath right through fields and woodland to the Hodge Close access road. Go left to Holme Ground. **7** Pass through the facing gate on the right rising to join the lateral bridleway, go left, northeast. After a fraction over 230 metres, a path branches right, up through the light birchwood, onto the open slope heading SSE direct to the summit. **8** Alternatively, continue with the bridleway a further 230 metres to a path, again right, passing up by evidence of small-scale slate quarrying which leads to a dam holding a lovely sheet of water. The path passes to the right, climbing easily to reach Uskdale Gap. This approach can also begin from the car park at Hodge Close quarry. In advance of this, walkers are encouraged to take hold of their courage and inspect the two monumental holes from within. Follow the road N through the cluster of dwellings; after Hodge Close Cottage find a track right, this leads via a gate, destination High Oxenfell Farm, but short of the gate, take the inviting path descending into the tree-shaded quarry,

Bluebells on the eastward descent from Uskdale Gap

Wetherlam from Raven Crag

Wetherlam Edge

Birk Fell

Hawk Rigg

Steel Edge

Birk Rigg

Tilberthwaite Ghyll

Penny Rigg Slate Mill

Low Tilberthwaite

right. Clamber over a chaos of boulders into the quarry depths to the awe-inspiring through cavern, supported by a stout pillar, from where get a view into the 'blue lagoon' of Hodge Close quarry *(see page 150)*. **9** One may walk right around the fell on tracks and quiet roads; the gated meadow way from Shepherd's Bridge to Yew Tree Farm; a useful link, as well as **10** the dale bottom path rising in harmony with the Skelwith/Coniston road to High Cross. To make the natural link with neighbouring Black Fell, follow the lovely Mountain Road east.

Yew Tree Tarn

Ivy Crag *(below)* and the summit from the north looking over Uskdale Gap

The Summit

A proud ridge with a short cliff to the east and cairns at either end, though the summit outcrop itself is has no cairn. For the best view of Yewdale *(left)*, venture to the cairn on the spur top of Raven Crag.

Safe Descents

Cue Uskdale Gap. Refrain from rambling about the rough plateau as there is no way down the E, S and W slopes. The nastiest trap lurks on the S with Calf and Raven Crags posing serious problems; neither is there access into the valley pastures along these fronts. Retreat to Uskdale Gap, then either go right for Yew Tree Tarn or left for Low Tilberthwaite.

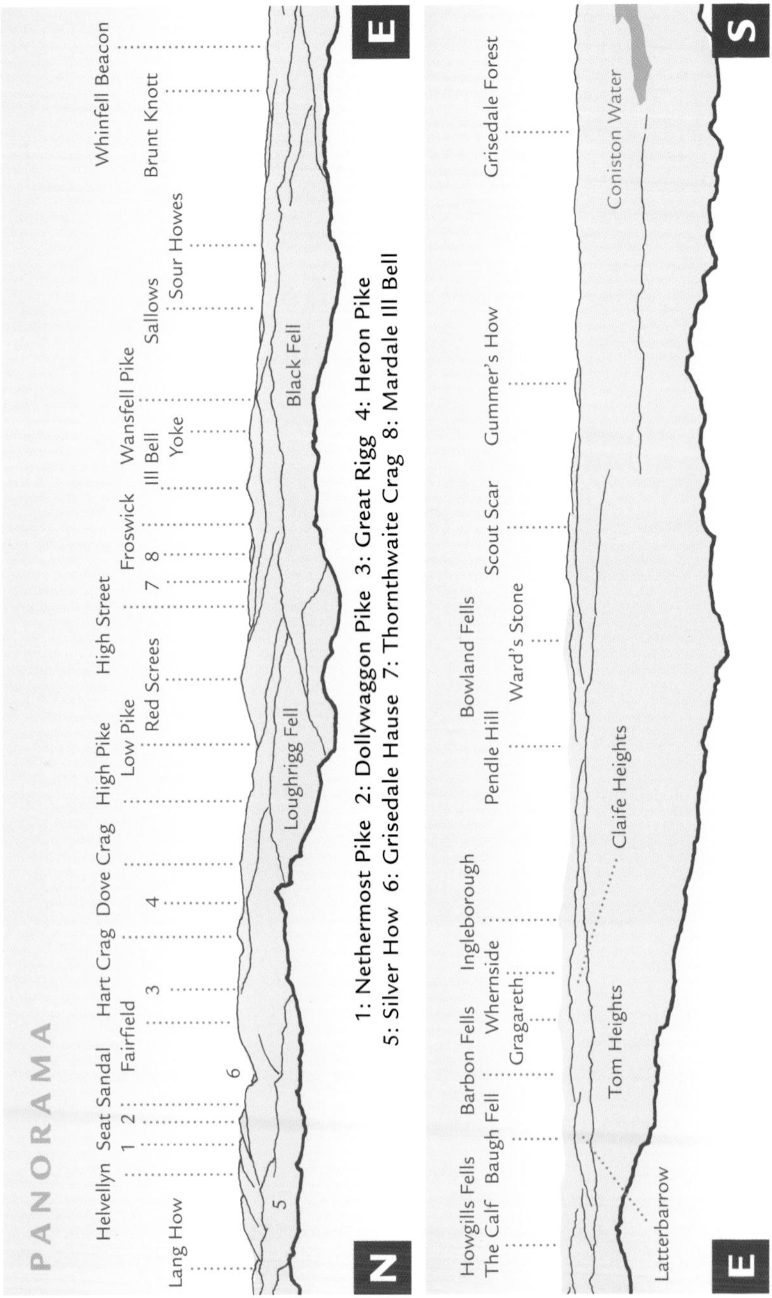

PANORAMA

E

Whinfell Beacon
Brunt Knott
Sour Howes
Sallows
Wansfell Pike
Black Fell
Ill Bell
Froswick
Yoke
High Street
8
7
Red Screes
Low Pike
High Pike
Loughrigg Fell
Dove Crag
Hart Crag
Seat Sandal
Fairfield
Helvellyn
Lang How
1
2
3
4
6
5

N

1: Nethermost Pike 2: Dollywaggon Pike 3: Great Rigg 4: Heron Pike
5: Silver How 6: Grisedale Hause 7: Thornthwaite Crag 8: Mardale Ill Bell

S

Grisedale Forest
Coniston Water
Gummer's How
Scout Scar
Ward's Stone
Bowland Fells
Pendle Hill
Claife Heights
Ingleborough
Whernside
Gragareth
Barbon Fells
Baugh Fell
The Calf
Howgills Fells
Tom Heights
Latterbarrow

E

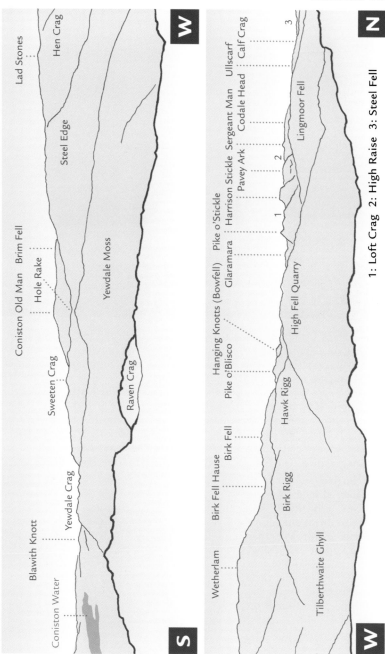

N

Lad Stones · Hen Crag

W

Steel Edge

Coniston Old Man · Brim Fell · Hole Rake

Sweeten Crag

Yewdale Moss

Raven Crag

Blawith Knott · Yewdale Crag

Coniston Water

S

Pike o'Stickle · Harrison Stickle · Sergeant Man · Ullscarf · Calf Crag
Pavey Ark · Codale Head
3
2
1

Hanging Knotts (Bowfell) · Glaramara · Pike o'Blisco

Lingmoor Fell

High Fell Quarry

Hawk Rigg

Birk Fell Hause · Birk Fell

Birk Rigg

Wetherlam

Tilberthwaite Ghyll

W

1: Loft Crag 2: High Raise 3: Steel Fell

MUNCASTER FELL

While Black Combe is often considered the seaboard fell, no other fell in the Lake District better serves to show the link between land and sea than Muncaster Fell. The moist air of the prevailing southwesterlies and 30 inches of rainfall per annum permits cereals to be grown on the coastal fringe. The rising rainfall gragh encourges beef cattle in a succulent pastoral landsape up to the high fells, above which the 120 inches of rainfall per annum imposes a climate and farming regime where only the hardy Herdwick can eke an existence. All of Britain reflects the effect of the Atlantic, but here we may witness the transition zones at an amazing glance. The fell is so very evidently a marine bridgehead.

Of further significance, this low, elongated ridge of wet moorland has been a bridgehead of another kind. Whether marauding or colonising, over many millennia people have made their first footfall into the Cumbrian hinterland on

Glannoventa bath-house

231 *metres*   758 *feet*

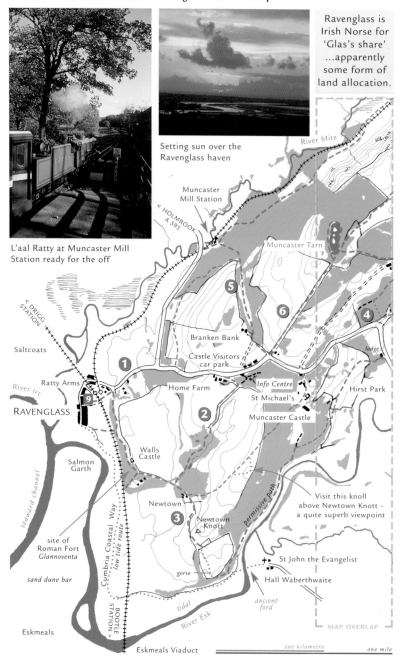

Ravenglass is
Irish Norse for
'Glas's share'
...apparently
some form of
land allocation.

Setting sun over the
Ravenglass haven

L'aal Ratty at Muncaster Mill
Station ready for the off

River Mite

Muncaster
Mill Station

< HOLMROOK
A 595

Muncaster Tarn

5

6

4

< DRIGG
STATION

Branken Bank

Castle Visitors
car park

Info Centre

lodge

Saltcoats

1

Home Farm

St Michael's

Hirst Park

Ratty Arms

River Irt

9

Muncaster Castle

RAVENGLASS

2

Walls
Castle

Salmon
Garth

Newtown

3

Newtown
Knott

permissive path

Visit this knoll
above Newtown Knott -
a quite superb viewpoint

seaward channel

Cumbria Coastal Way
low tide route

site of
Roman Fort
Glannoventa

gorse

St John the Evangelist

sand dune bar

Hall Waberthwaite

ancient
ford

tidal

MAP OVERLAP

BOOTLE

Eskmeals

River Esk

Eskmeals Viaduct

one kilometre

one mile

Ideally the footpath
next to the railway
would connect to
the Bowerhouse
...*that's a Mite
good idea!*

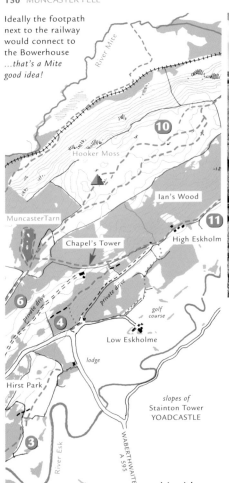

Malcolm Guyatt standing on one of
his highly individual and personally
purpose-built footbridges in front of
the Eskmeals Viaduct, with
Muncaster Fell rising beyond. In his
capacity of National Park Ranger,
Malcolm has been caring for the wel-
fare of South-West Lakeland for thir-
ty-two years. In fact, he was appoint-
ed the year I wandered up Stainton
Pike with Wainwright.

this ridge, coming up from the ancient harbour at Ravenglass. Bronze Age and later
relics abound, from Swinside Stone Circle to Barnscar 'city'. The
Romans certainly valued the haven, establishing Glannoventa as an
important west coast approach to their northern frontier. Later settlers,
most notably the Vikings from the Isle of Man and Ireland, found shore
here and quickly headed for the hills, establishing their own brand of
farming, surviving in place-names and settlement patterns to this day.
So the walker, wandering alone on the wild and wet of Muncaster Fell,
may sense an ancient footfall in every stride. On either side of this narrow fell, from Ravenglass to Eskdale Green, are lush valleys drained by
the rivers Esk and Mite, thus isolating the fell from any natural bond
with either the Western, Mid-Western or Southern Fells. These rivers,

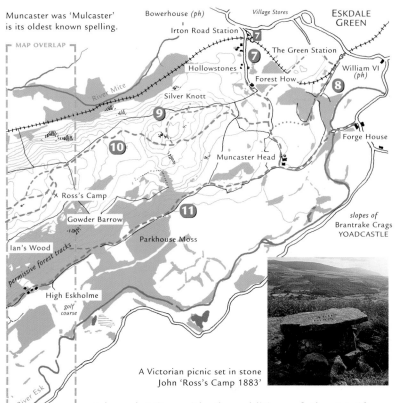

Muncaster was 'Mulcaster' is its oldest known spelling.

MAP OVERLAP

Bowerhouse *(ph)*

Village Stores

ESKDALE GREEN

Irton Road Station

7

The Green Station

7

Hollowstones

Forest How

William VI *(ph)*

8

River Mite

Silver Knott

9

Forge House

10

Muncaster Head

X Ross's Camp

11

Gowder Barrow

slopes of Brantrake Crags YOADCASTLE

Ian's Wood

Parkhouse Moss

permissive forest tracks

High Eskholme

golf course

River Esk

A Victorian picnic set in stone John 'Ross's Camp 1883'

Esk and Mite, with the addition of the Irt (from Wasdale), recoil at the point of entry into the sea, halted by the massive sand bar dunes at the fell's western tip. This quirky estuary ensures that almost all the rain on the high Scafells is brought together before entry into the sea, making the most certain of harbours. The dune landscape of Drigg and Eskmeals are high-value wildlife habitats and unique in Cumbria.

Out to sea the Isle of Man, composed of rocks linked with the Lakes, is at its closest, Douglas being just 38 miles from Ravenglass as the gull flies. Three man-made features make Muncaster Fell irresistible: Ravenglass village, a special area of conservation with its access to the estuary shore and Walls Castle; Muncaster Castle and dear L'aal Ratty. The miniature railway, with its trains' distinctive dry hoot, brings back the joy of gentle travel through the loveliest of landscapes and offers a happy combination of ride and stride: travel out with the the train, walk back upon the fell for the perfect summer's day outing. Indeed there are four fell-foot stations giving flexibility to your walk plan, Ravenglass, Muncaster Mill, Irton Road and the Green.

ASCENT *from Ravenglass*

Use the generous village car park GR 085965. **1** For walkers earnest to reach the fell (or backtracking following the ridge route traverse from Eskdale Green), follow a footway up from the village by the war memorial to the junction with the A595, continuing on, by the public entrance to Muncaster Castle grounds, to the sharp right-hand bend, here the bridle-lane onto the ridge, Fell Lane, begins.

2 Cross the main-line footbridge south of the station to a hand-gate and the roadway by the Walls caravan park. Go right, where a newly created footway weaves by a woodland fringe alongside the Muncaster Estate road. Take a moment at the English Heritage enclosure to inspect the remarkable remains of Walls Castle. Claimed to be the tallest wholly Roman building in northern Britain, the regular stone coursing is authentic, the rendering may be later. The associated Roman harbour fort of Glannoventa is only visible as a vallum feature in the enclosure across the roadway. The bath-house contains a statue niche reminiscent of Chesters (Cilurnum) on Hadrian's Wall. Two rooms remain with a blocked hypocaust flue visible at the base of the south wall *(at the figure's feet in the image on page 148)*. The building survives because it found use long after the Romans withdrew. Probably set within a timber structure, it carries legendary links with Avallach, the Celtic Lord of the Underworld. Continue south, trees inhibiting any chance of a seaward view, though one may reach this point from the village at low tide along the shore. A 'Muncaster, Knotts End and Newtown' sign directs left, along a drive. Approaching buildings, a further left turn leads up a track by a recently created pond. The fenced lane enters the tree belt; either go left to Home Farm or continue into the Castle grounds beside the circular Muncaster Interactive building and the Sino-Himalayan Garden. Go left to the crenellated gateway to the A595 (locked at 5.30pm). By either route go right along the roadside footway to the sharp right-hand bend to enter Fell Lane.

3 An intriguing and very pleasant alternative is to continue on the foot-path, signed 'Cumbria Coastal Way', through Newtown Farm and then beneath Newtown Knott, surmounted by an old navigation tower. Crossing pasture, enter woodland at a hand-gate, coming close to the bridle-path along the Esk shore *(above)*, almost opposite the Hall Waberthwaite ford. Go left upstream on a permissive path to enter Croft Coppice, and beneath the tree-screened Muncaster Castle, ancient home of the Penningtons, onto the drive traversing Hirst Park to Hirst Lodge. The family inheritance has long been handed down by the female line, hence when Patrick Gordon-Duff married into the family, the impressive triple-barrelled Gordon-Duff-Pennington was created! It is highly plausable. that the castle rests upon the site of a Roman mansio residence. The name 'caster' implies a fortified site, the situation is perfect, sheltered from the Irish Sea (Celtic Sea). **4** Follow the minimally verged A595, taking the second right (bridleway sign), at the tight left-hand bend; after 36 metres find decking, left. A permissive path, up the untrammelled wooded bank, reaches a lateral woodland track near a grand old spreading oak. Go right, the track is prone

to dampness. Pass beneath Chapel's Tower; as a wall gateway nears, the path is ushered left to a ladder-stile into the rising path from Eskholme to Muncaster Tarn. Piercing the woodland like a rocket, Chapel's Tower *(right)* is a folly built on the site of an ancient tree where King Henry VI was discovered hiding after defeat at the battle of Towton, near Hexham. Having enjoyed a few days hospitality, the grateful monarch presented his host with a decorated green glass bowl adorned with gold and enamel, offering a blessing that family fortunes would be secure as long as the bowl remained intact. Needless to say only a replica is held in the castle, the vaulted original is kept cradled in cotton wool! The pepper-pot tower was built to mark the continuance of this 'Luck of Muncaster'.

5 A delightful bridleway ascends from the Muncaster Mill Station within woodland, joining the access track from Branken Wall Farm to meet the main road at the foot of Fell Lane.

6 Fell Lane *(right)* is the focus of all ascents from the west. Even the Eskholme and Chapel Wood paths draw up to join forces at Muncaster Tarn. There is a gate halfway up, otherwise it's plain sailing to the rhododendron canopy

close to the tarn. Make a point of visiting this secret pool, indulge yourself upon the circuit path to sample its 'far from the madding crowd' tranquillity; lillies grow in the southwestern corner, in a wet season the tarn overflows at both ends! The track heads on up by a gate onto the undulating fell, passing gorse. The path forks at the forest corner, the continuing path avoids the summit altogether, and much of the damper ground for that matter. The summit is irresistible, the stronger path steps up the short bank left and heads for Hooker Crag.

The ridge east from Hooker Crag looking to Scafell, Bowfell and Crinkle Crags

ASCENT *from Eskdale Green*

A smart move for summer Ratty riders: park in Ravenglass, enjoy the trip all the way to Dalegarth, perhaps taking lunch there; returning, alight at either the Green or Irton Road Stations, for a fine backtracking traverse of the scenically special Muncaster Fell ridge. **7** The ridge path is most easily and swiftly gained from Irton Road Station GR 137000. Cross the railway bridge and follow the no through road, with its pleasing views into Eskdale, to end at Forest How. The green bridleway skirts the garden hedge to the right to slip through a gate onto a track with dense gorse to the right. The ridge path branches right, short of a stile/gate. **8** The Green Station GR 145998 makes a neat country walk approach; a narrow path leads west directly from the platform to a stile midst a ford, with stepping stones. Rise on a firm path holding to the wall beside woodland. From its right-hand corner, which can be cattle muddied, traverse the pasture with the short bank close left to meet up with the bridleway from Muncaster Head at the stile/gate, mentioned above. **9** The ridge walk may ensue, the path hugs the gorse (sounds painful, but is not obligatory!) to reach a kissing-gate. A few paces further the path swings left on a steady stone-edged rise, an apparently outmoded television aerial is prominent on the headland up to the right.

10 As a ploy to take fullest benefit of the utterly gorgeous eastern view into Eskdale, keep to the lesser path straight up through the bracken, keeping close to the ridge wall. At the top the briefest of breaches in this

Looking to the Coniston Fells from the ridge east of Hooker Crag

fell-wall permits access to the Silver Knott bluff – the name might allude to silver birch, which makes quite an appearance on this quarter of the fell. A sheep trod leads south, away from the wall, just missing the highest ground. Descend the bracken bank by a large holly tree to join the incline ridge path. The main path heads west, cornering the headland, dipping down an incline to traverse a birch-dappled hollow before rising to come close to the ridge wall, in so doing negotiating much damp ground. The gateway in the wall corner does not spell an end of soggy going, the path is immediately forced to make an exaggerated leftward sweep around a marsh. Some walkers head on (bound for the

The tree-lined Esk backed by Muncaster Head and Silver Knott from Brant Rake

summit) climbing the prominent bank, while others angle on left to come by the collapsing stable stone inscribed 'Ross's Camp 1883', installed to mark the favourite viewpoint of John Ross, agent of the Muncastle Castle estate. The situation is simply splendid, a veritable feast for the eyes. The continuing path is firm but has one drawback, it misses the summit completely! However, the path mounting the bank, passing a large prominent boulder, snakes irresistibly along the ridge, skirts the few knolls flanking Hooker Moss to climb solidly onto Hooker Crag. The name actually means 'hollow marsh' [hol-kerr]; indeed locals always call Holker Hall, near Cartmel, 'Hooker Hall'.

11 After the elation of the ridge path, many walkers will value the opportunity to complete their walk in circular fashion, on foot, applying their minds to a train of thought rather than to rest on a train seat. At present there is no continuous path along the shady scarp base beside L'aal Ratty, maybe one day... However, a bridle-lane leading along the sunny southern foot of the fell via Muncaster Head and High Eskholme (golf club grounds) provides the perfect contrast to the moorland traverse, wooded much of the way, interrupted by just one gate at High Eskholme itself. Walkers have liberty in the woodlands, though few exercise it. Immediately west of High Eskholme the right-of-way splits, forsaking the metalled roadway. The more useful option draws up right by sheds, a steady well-graded path mounting to be joined at a ladder-stile by the permissive path out of Chapel Wood (route **6**). It passes within 100 metres and within sight of Chapel's Tower, passing through a hand-gate en route to meet the top of Fell Lane at the dam of Muncaster Tarn, a place of reflections *(below)*.

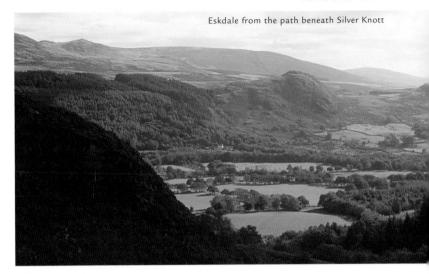

Eskdale from the path beneath Silver Knott

The Summit

A fine stone-built OS pillar, constructed in the distinctive Eskdale granite, graces the top of Hooker Crag. There is ample scope to sit and glory in a wonderful panorama, a heady cocktail of mountain and maritime. Indeed, this is the nearest Lakeland fell summit to the Isle of Man. Even if two parties met on the top, they could lay claim to their own section of the summit knoll and remain oblivious of the other.

Safe Descents

The course is quite simply put: there is no way to north or south off the ridge from the open fell. Steep path-less scarp, most richly wooded on the south side, proffer no appropriate links with recognised paths on either hand. There are, in effect, two ridge paths; that from the summit is obvious enough, though the east-ward trail weaves more laboriously towards the valley base of Eskdale Green. The west-bound path quickly leads to the shelter and security of woodland by Muncaster Tarn and Fell Lane, en route for the village of Ravenglass, only 2.5 miles distant from the summit.

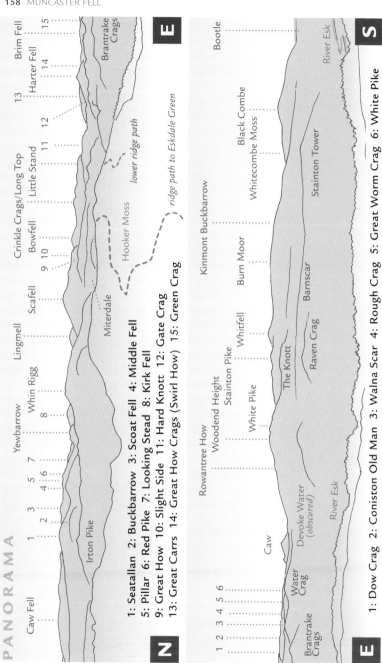

PANORAMA

Caw Fell · Brim Fell · Harter Fell · 13 · 12 · 11 · Crinkle Crags/Long Top · Little Stand · 9 10 · Bowfell · Scafell · Lingmell · Yewbarrow · Whin Rigg · 8 · 7 · 5 6 · 4 · 3 · 2 · 1

Brantrake Crags · lower ridge path · ridge path to Eskdale Green · Hooker Moss · Miterdale · Irton Pike

E

1: Seatallan 2: Buckbarrow 3: Scoat Fell 4: Middle Fell
5: Pillar 6: Red Pike 7: Looking Stead 8: Kirk Fell
9: Great How 10: Slight Side 11: Hard Knott 12: Gate Crag
13: Great Carrs 14: Great How Crags (Swirl How) 15: Green Crag

N

Bootle · Black Combe · Whitecombe Moss · Kinmont Buckbarrow · Burn Moor · Whitfell · Stainton Pike · Woodend Height · Rowantree How · White Pike · Caw

River Esk · Stainton Tower · Barnscar · Raven Crag · The Knott · Devoke Water (obscured) · River Esk · Water Crag · Brantrake Crags · 1 2 · 3 4 5 · 6

S

E

1: Dow Crag 2: Coniston Old Man 3: Walna Scar 4: Rough Crag 5: Great Worm Crag 6: White Pike

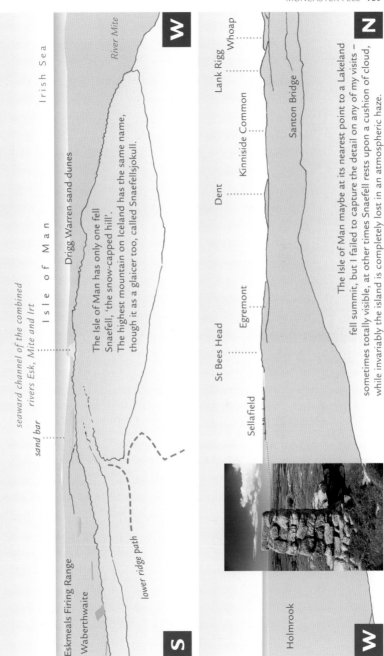

W

River Mite

Irish Sea

Isle of Man

Drigg Warren sand dunes

seaward channel of the combined
rivers Esk, Mite and Irt

sand bar

The Isle of Man has only one fell
Snaefell, 'the snow-capped hill'.
The highest mountain on Iceland has the same name,
though it as a glacier too, called Snaefellsjokull.

Eskmeals Firing Range
Waberthwaite

lower ridge path

S

N

Whoap
Lank Rigg

Kinniside Common

Dent

Santon Bridge

Egremont

St Bees Head

Sellafield

Holmrook

W

The Isle of Man maybe at its nearest point to a Lakeland
fell summit, but I failed to capture the detail on any of my visits –
sometimes totally visible, at other times Snaefell rests upon a cushion of cloud,
while invariably the island is completely lost in an atmospheric haze.

STAINTON PIKE 16

The fell nestles into the eastern skyline of the southwestern fells along-side Yoadcastle; from the A595 you sense one fell mass, each top players on the stage of a modest fell drama. To pick out the Pike as a solitary objective, witness it from Corney Fell Road, above the junction with the A595 at Millgate. The Knott *(below)* showing the fell's cleanest profile, is emphasised again during the bridleway walk in by the home-stead site *(right)*. But from most other vantage points it has little form, merging into the vast moorland bowl of Storthes to the east.

Apart from the summit, interest lies in the fragmentary remains of early settlement encountered on a roving ramble, the impressive gorge of Rowantree Force and the shining level of Holehouse Tarn. For the record, Hole House lies at the foot of Storthes, on the Duddon side of the fell. To judge by the ridge path, walkers traversing from Whitfell to Woodend Height tend to ignore Stainton Pike, most remiss.

498 *metres* 1,634 *feet*

The homestead, Dark Age in origin, can be identified by a ring of boulders

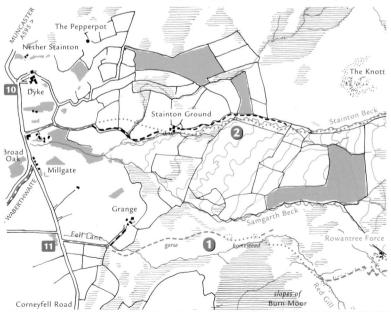

The Brown Cow, on the A595 at Waberthwaite, Lane End, is the nearest pub for post-walk refreshment... it comes with the author's 'taste test' commendation.

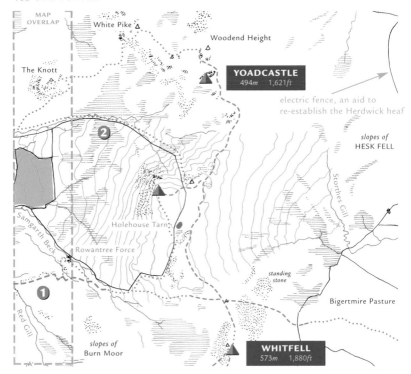

MAP OVERLAP

White Pike △

Woodend Height

YOADCASTLE
494m 1,621ft

The Knott

electric fence, an aid to
re-establish the Herdwick heaf

slopes of
HESK FELL

Storthes Gill

Samgarth Beck

Holehouse Tarn

Rowantree Force

standing
stone

Bigertmire Pasture

Red Gill

slopes of
Burn Moor

WHITFELL
573m 1,880ft

These two pictures are dedicated to my happy memories of
Alfred Wainwright — for his inspiration and encouragement.

This faded B&W image of Rowantree Force was one of my earliest fellwalking photographs: taken in the autumn of 1972 whilst standing next to AW during one of our numerous expeditions together, on that occasion during research for his *The Outlying Fells of Lakeland* guide. Returning to this out of the way spot had great poignance for me.

AW had a huge impact on my life at that time, following my discovery of his Pictorial Guides — beautifully crafted books that will live on as an enduring record of one man's love affair with the fells. The publication of this present guide, within the Lakeland Fellranger series, appropriately coincides with the fiftieth anniversary of the publication of AW's first guidebook, *The Eastern Fells*.

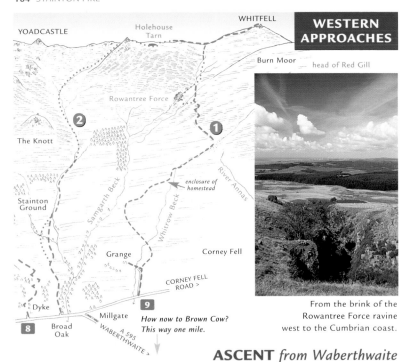

WESTERN APPROACHES

YOADCASTLE — Holehouse Tarn — WHITFELL

Burn Moor — head of Red Gill

Rowantree Force

The Knott

enclosure of homestead

River Annas

Stainton Ground

Samgarth Beck

Whitrow Beck

Grange — Corney Fell

Corney Fell

CORNEY FELL ROAD >

Dyke — Millgate — *How now to Brown Cow? This way one mile.*

8 Broad Oak — WABERTHWAITE — A 595 — WABERTHWAITE >

9

From the brink of the Rowantree Force ravine west to the Cumbrian coast.

ASCENT *from Waberthwaite*

Park on the verge just beyond the entrance to Fell Lane. **1** Follow the lane, ignore the cattle-grid, pass through the facing gate. The bridle-track embarks on a winding course across a rough pasture of rushes and gorse, no more than an intermittent path after the ford, sometimes in doubt, but continuing eastward between Samgarth and Whitrow Becks. Finding drier ground, draw alongside Whitrow Beck, wander through the cryptic homestead enclosure. A more certain path angles right, keeping company with the gullied ground at the foot of Red Gill. A cairn indicates the start of a grooved path left, partially lined with boulders, zig-zagging as the ground steepens. To visit Rowantree Force, slip through the adjacent bouldery hollow left, passing a small ruined fold to venture into the ravine's midst. If you follow the ravine edge upstream, by the time you regain the bridleway, it is already becoming indistinct as it skirts the Withe Bottom mire. For ease of walking, keep up left beside the fence, cross over Sergeant Crag, and as the fell levels, cross the fence close to Holehouse Tarn. A spidery path leads NW to the summit knoll.

2 The ascent via Stainton Beck is the natural descent on a round trip. Park by the telephone kiosk opposite Broad Oak Farm, cross the cattle-grid, and follow the farm access to Stainton Ground. Although a foot-path, complete with stiles is available, it is preferable to follow the farm

Stainton Pike SE aspect

track – unless you wish to wade through the knee-high water at the Black Beck ford. Cross a ladder-stile right and an unusually broad foot-bridge immediately before the farmyard gate. Embark on a footpath that hugs Stainton Beck by two fence stiles; pass the environs of Stainton Ground, continuing with gorse and cattle-poached marshy ground for cold comfort. By two ladder-stiles and an intermediate low fence stile reach the open fell, now pathless; beat the bracken. Keep with the right-hand fence, climbing to the saddle, just east of the summit; cross the fence to reach the cairn.

The Summit

A broad north/south ridge gains focus on a modest outcrop NW of Holehouse Tarn, a splendid flourish of rock surmounted with a neat edifice befitting a pike. Be sure to linger and enjoy your time on top.

Safe Descents

With a fence straddling the plateau close at hand there is some assurance in mist, but only if you have a western destination in mind. The footpath by Stainton Beck is invisible and painfully rough in places.

Ridge Routes to....

WHITFELL	DESCENT 20*ft*	ASCENT 250*ft*	1 mile
YOADCASTLE	DESCENT 220*ft*	ASCENT 190*ft*	1.2 miles

Re-cross the plain fence to join the narrow ridge path running E of Holehouse Tarn, N to Yoadcastle and S to Whitfell, it's that simple!

PANORAMA

1 2 3 4 5 6 7 8 9 10 11 12 13 14 15 16 17 18 19 20 21 22 23 24 25 26 27

Woodend Height

Yoadcastle

Great How

Green Crag

Hesk Fell

28

N   **E**

1: Scoat Fell 2: Red Pike 3: Pillar 4: Illgill Head 5: Black Sail Pass 6: Robinson 7: Kirk Fell
8: Brandreth 9: Great Gable 10: Scafell 11: Scafell Pike 12: Esk Hause 13: Esk Pike 14: Bowfell
15: Crinkle Crags 16: Little Stand 17: Harter Fell 18: Dove Crag 19: Great Carrs 20: Grey Friar
21: Swirl How 22: Levers Hause 23: Brim Fell 24: Dow Crag 25: Coniston Old Man 26: Brown Pike
27: Walna Scar 28: Great Worm Crag

Burn Moor

Whitfell

Holehouse Tarn

Kirkby Moor

Bowland Fells

Ingleborough

Stickle Pike

Fox Haw

The Pike

S   **E**

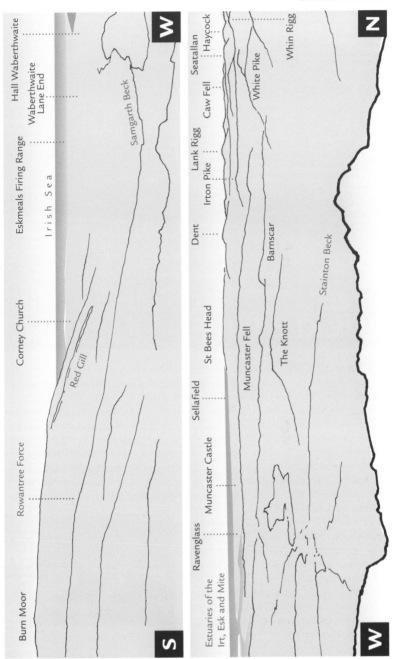

W

Hall Waberthwaite
Waberthwaite Lane End
Eskmeals Firing Range
I r i s h   S e a
Samgarth Beck
Corney Church
Red Gill
Rowantree Force
Burn Moor
S

N

Seatallan
Haycock
Caw Fell
White Pike
Whin Rigg
Lank Rigg
Irton Pike
Dent
Barnscar
St Bees Head
Muncaster Fell
Stainton Beck
The Knott
Sellafield
Muncaster Castle
Ravenglass
Estuaries of the
Irt, Esk and Mite
W

STICKLE PIKE 17

The hamlet of Hall Dunnerdale lies in the Duddon valley. While the Dunnerdale Fells are identified as being the southwestern slopes of Stickle Pike, but hey, Dunnerdale Beck flows into the River Lickle at Broughton Mills. Surely this side valley is the real Dunnerdale, while over the watershed the main valley, in the singular, is the Duddon. Whatever their names, both are beautiful, made the more so by the shapely presence of Stickle Pike and its contingent of associated tops. In keeping with the confusion, the parallel ridge, enclosing the Dunnerdale Beck valley, actually contains a higher summit, Fox Haw, superior by 29 feet in old money, 10 metres in new. How many walkers remember the heights of fells anyway? They will Stickle Pike, if they can count to four, and Great Stickle, from which they may comprehend the rise of land from sea-level to a neat 1,000 feet! Most visitors are content to pick off the fell blithely from the open road summit at Kiln Bank Cross, but there is a good deal more to appreciate... read on MacDuff.

Blacksmith's Arms, Broughton Mills

376 metres   1,234 feet

Stickle Pike means
'the steep peak'

slopes of
GREAT WORM CRAG

< BIRKER FELL
ROAD

slopes of
The Pike
HESK FELL

PO/shop

St John's

ULPHA

River Duddon

HALL DUNNERDALE

Duddon Valley

Kiln Bank

Brock Barrow

slopes of
CAW

Park Head Road

Fox Haw
385mtrs 1,263ft

old
quarries

23

Stickle Tarn

7

1

old
quarry

2

Hoses

Raven's
Crag

Low Birks

Yow Pike

slate
mine

Tarn
Hill

Hare
Hall

Stainton
Ground

22

Dunnerdale Fells

Great
Stickle
305mtrs
1,000ft

Dunnerdale Beck

The Knott

3

Little
Stickle

4

6

Ulpha
Park

Stonestar

Scrithwaite

bench

5

Hovel
Knott

Green Bank

BROUGHTON
MILLS

24

TORVER >

Cat's Crag

Raven's Crag

Hawes

Pickthall
Ground

Blacksmith's
Arms (PH)

Low Whineray Ground

DUDDON BRIDGE

River Lickle

< BROUGHTON
IN-FURNESS

Croglinhurst

one kilometre   one mile

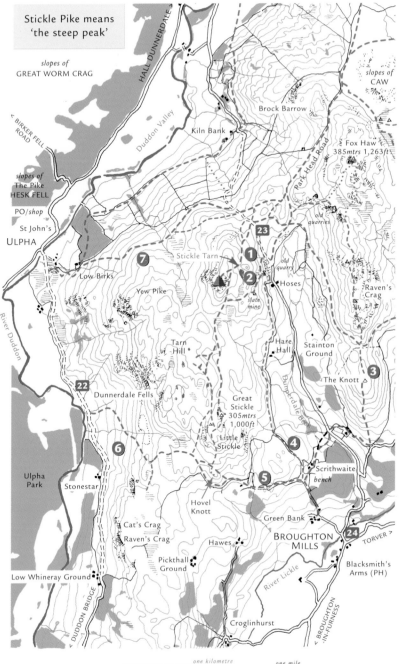

Fox Haw and Caw from Stickle Tarn

ASCENT *from Kiln Bank Cross*

1 'Get me crocodile sandwiches and make them snappy...' Well, this ascent is snappy all right, and if you have an even number in your party you may climb crocodile fashion too! Park at Kiln Bank Cross and follow the via tuta (beaten path) curving up the shallow combe from south to southwest. The ground steepens, Stickle Tarn does its level best to hide, but seek it out to enjoy a moment's quiet contemplation at this basin oasis. The eroded path strewn with loose stone inhibits a flowing stride to the top. **2** An interesting variant ascent begins 230 metres down the road, where a slate miners' incline bears right, slanting up the bracken bank to a mine level; pass up right by a workshop ruin to join the ridge path emanating from Great Stickle. Cut up to link with the direct route at a high saddle.

ASCENT *from Broughton Mills*

3 The fell has obvious circular route potential, in pole position the horse-shoe Dunnerdale Beck skyline walk. Take it anti-clockwise from the Blacksmith's Arms – the perfect den for any denizen to return to: real ales, scrumptious food in a setting of stone-flagged floors, wooden panelling, old tables and open fires. Either follow the road crossing the Lickle; take two right turns to reach the ladder-stile at the foot of the Knott ridge. Or go left via Green Bank, the rustic Scrithwaite, crossing the clapper footbridge, then the dale road. Cross into the lane approach to and through Knott End, via gates, to reach that ladder-stile.

A clear path leads up the ridge through the early bracken onto the brow of the Knott, with a cairn almost on the highest point *(left)*. The ridge path is pursued north, crossing a broken wall and the bridle-path in the saddle. One can follow this drove-way left, contouring directly to Kiln Bank Cross. Skyliners keep up the broken edge ahead, drawing by a rock-girt pool onto Raven's Crag. Strategically sited cairns mark good viewpoints *(below)* overlooking the white-washed Hoses to Stickle Pike. The ridge path dwindles at a depres-

sion; the route onto the raised headland of Fox Haw is undefined. Again the summit rock rib has a cairn with a view to merit the effort, to Stickle Pike, with the peak of Caw in particular, seen to good effect *(bottom)*.

Descend the southern slopes, joining an old quarry track associated with the two large gaping hollows of the old Stainton Ground slate quarry. This slate is hard and differs markedly from its Welsh counterpart, not forming smooth regular plane surfaces. Notice the holly growing from the mouth of the

lower level. Join the Park Head Road green-way, a useful approach route to Stickle Pike from Seathwaite. After 90 metres branch up right, leaving the track, which otherwise leads to the road-gate at Hoses. Pass a slate mine level – internal railings preventing entry into what appears to be a nasty black hole – to reach the open parking space at Kiln Bank Cross.

4 The Green Bank route passes via a cottage into the edge of woodland, emerging at a hand-gate. It rises to fine viewpoint thoughtfully provided with a wooden picnic bench and the favoured views down the Lickle valley to the coast. Either follow the footpath rising north via a broken walled lane, entering the fell enclosure at a gate from where it accompanies the intake wall, brushing through rank bracken above Hare Hall to join the road at Hoses. **5** The skyline option bears left from the bench, the walled lane rising and dipping to a gate, with stone stoups adjacent *(left)*. The trackway passes by a stone hovel (barn), rising to a gate. The continuing green track sweeps around Hovel Knott, but the prime route branches up through the bracken on a clear path. Aim for the saddle to the right of Hovel Knott: a lovely little viewpoint in its own right. Bear up right from the narrow col; a path weaves over Little Stickle to the fading white-washed OS pillar on Great Stickle: a handsome view-point for the lower Duddon and Lickle valleys. The northward ridge connection to Stickle Pike *(right)* has two basic variations, either forge swiftly on the slightly lower level, traversing the marshy hollow, or hold more crisply to the ridge, pass-ing the various attractive pools and puddles that characterise Tarn Hill.

Stickle Pike from Great Stickle

ASCENT *from Ulpha*

There are various small parking places where the rocky river and open road come close. Visitors of all ages revel in this lovely stretch of free-flowing water, not seen so well since Cockley Beck. The rough skyline of Yew Pike shields Stickle Pike, giving no hint of a comfortable walk. Two paths make effective connections with the spine of the ridge. Both fend off the all too evident bracken with unexpected ease, combined they make a really good scenic circular walk. **6** The footpath from Broughton Mills, crossing over the ridge by Hovel Knott, has its Duddon roots at GR 201917. A signed path stepping off the road by a small gill bridge weaves up the fellside, the lovely way drifting right. As the climb eases, skirt a hollow angling left into the ridge-top saddle north of Great Stickle.

7 A strip of tarmac leads from the valley road close to the old school, rising to the attractively located cottage at Low Birks. There are two bridle-paths: that on the open fell, setting course for Kiln Bank Cross, provides the most marvellous exhibition of the Duddon valley, a definite five-star parade. To follow this mount the bank by the water tank with the wall left. Veer away from the wall to negotiate damp ground, the path briefly indistinct. The worn way, restored underfoot, passes a large quartz-streaked outcrop. Soon after fording a head-stream amid light juniper, the path splits indistinctly, the more apparent path coming by the wall to meet the road just above the cattle-grid sign and therefore on the Duddon side of the road pass. Go right to complete the ascent.

The Summit

No wonder people race up from the road pass. It's a lovely little summit, with two tops, offering a view that would cheer anyone up.

Safe Descents

Cheer you may, but don't treat the descent with frivolity. Keep tight to the one way up as the one way down, especially to the first shoulder.

Ridge Route to...

CAW   DESCENT *490ft*   ASCENT *990ft*   2.3 miles
Follow the popular path N to the open road at Kiln Bank Cross. Head straight across with one of two green paths leading NE down to the Park Head Road bridleway. Coming alongside a wall, after the bridleway from Long Mire merges from the right. Watch for the obvious Caw quarry slate miners' incline branching right. Ascend to the mine, climb the rake directly above, to progress to the OS pillar on the ultimate rock.

PANORAMA

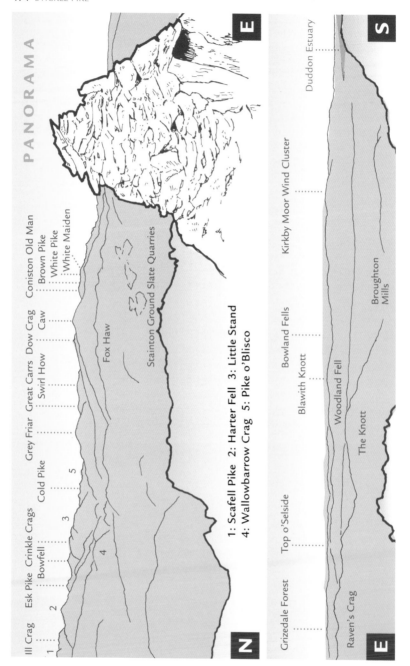

E

N

Ill Crag
Esk Pike
Crinkle Crags
Bowfell
Grey Friar
Great Carrs
Swirl How
Cold Pike
Dow Crag
Caw
Coniston Old Man
Brown Pike
White Pike
White Maiden

1
2
3
4
5

Fox Haw

Stainton Ground Slate Quarries

1: Scafell Pike 2: Harter Fell 3: Little Stand
4: Wallowbarrow Crag 5: Pike o'Blisco

S

E

Duddon Estuary

Kirkby Moor Wind Cluster

Bowland Fells

Blawith Knott

Broughton
Mills

Woodland Fell

The Knott

Top o'Selside

Grizedale Forest

Raven's Crag

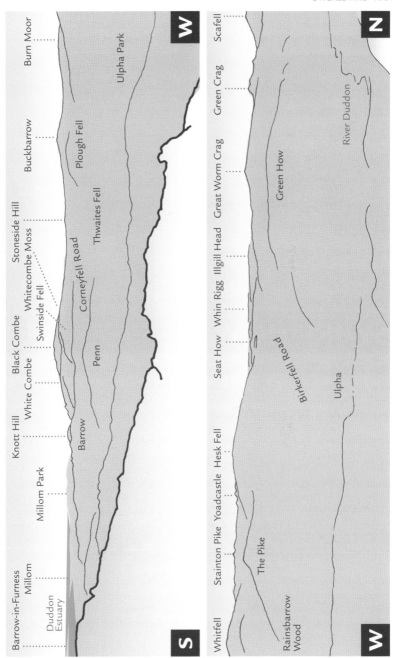

W

Burn Moor
Buckbarrow
Stoneside Hill
Whitecombe Moss
Black Combe
Knott Hill
White Combe
Swinside Fell
Millom Park
Barrow-in-Furness
Millom
Duddon Estuary

Ulpha Park
Plough Fell
Thwaites Fell
Corneyfell Road
Penn
Barrow

S

N

Scafell
Green Crag
Great Worm Crag
Illgill Head
Whin Rigg
Seat How
Hesk Fell
Yoadcastle
Stainton Pike
Whitfell

River Duddon
Green How
Birkerfell Road
Ulpha
The Pike
Rainsbarrow Wood

W

The Old Man gets the plaudits and crowds, Swirl How principally gets the genuine fellwalker. Plus the nod in height, by a meagre metre. But an inch is as good as a mile for those marking up their fells with the focal summit of the Coniston group, from where three major ridges swirl. The ridge that climbs out of Little Langdale with its high connection with the Mid-Western Fells on Wrynose Pass, considered part and parcel of Great Carrs, in truth has its ultimate goal upon Swirl How. Southward a spinal ridge drifts steadily, down to Levers Hause, en route to Brim Fell and the Old Man. While an exhilarating rock group, the Prison Band falls sternly eastward, the fell looks nothing from the west. While Wetherlam dominates northeastern perspectives, the summit forms a graceful peaked culmination to the Greenburn valley. The Prison Band aspect commands the ridge approach from Black Sails and, a personal favourite viewpoint, the top of Raven Tor on Brim Fell, from where Great How Crags dominate *(above)*. Great and Little How Crags are the exclusive preserve of rock climbers, hence the white-painted notice on the east side of Great How's crest, warning walkers off any thought of a descent. The wanderer, however, will find interesting the quest for the goose bield which is located tight under these crags, reached from the climbers' approach path above Levers Water.

804 *metres*   2,638 *feet*

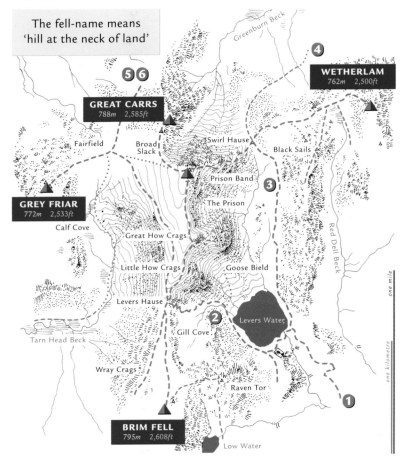

The fell-name means
'hill at the neck of land'

5 6

GREAT CARRS
788m   2,585ft

WETHERLAM
762m   2,500ft

4

Greenburn Beck

Fairfield

Broad
Slack

Swirl Hause

Black Sails

Prison Band

3

GREY FRIAR
772m   2,533ft

The Prison

Calf Cove

Great How Crags

Red Dell Beck

Little How Crags

Goose Bield

Levers Hause

Gill Cove

Levers Water

2

Tarn Head Beck

Wray Crags

Raven Tor

1

one mile

one kilometre

BRIM FELL
795m   2,608ft

Low Water

ASCENT *from Coniston, via the Coppermines valley*

1 The regular track, still industrially used by Burlington's slate-hauling
lorries and United Utilities vehicles, advances up the Church Beck valley
from Coniston. The level approach to the superbly sited Coppermines
Youth Hostel is followed by a brief steady rise, then, after the concrete
mass of the waterworks, pursue its zig-zags to the outflow of Levers
Water. Two routes to the summit are at once available, neither is preferable, both have merit, combining to form to a neat round trip.

2 Bear left, crossing the dam causeway, marching over the broken
ground associated with the old Simon's Nick copper mine workings; the
collapsed portion looks forbidding, and is, unless geared-up with ropes
for a proper speological investigation *(see page 49)*. The Boulder valley

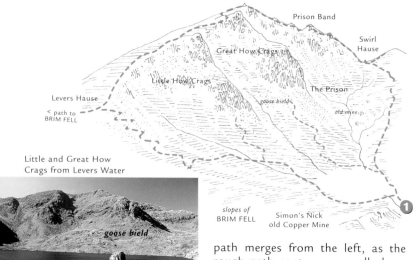

Little and Great How
Crags from Levers Water

goose bield

Reverse view of the above
from the top of Prison Band

Cotton-grass fringed
pool in the Prison

path merges from the left, as the rough path contours on well above the southern shore of Levers Water. The tarn-name suggests mine lifting gear, but clearly this is wrong. Perhaps it has common roots with Tarn at Leaves on Rosthwaite Fell, though the setting is altogether different and, as this tarn has been harnessed by mining interests, it has a bleaker countenance. Ford Cove Beck, with cairns now confirming a well-maintained path, climbs towards Levers Hause. But there is good reason to spur right to discover the goose bield situated on a shelf beneath the large boulders below Great How Crags. Reach it via the left-hand side of a shallow rigg, which is more particularly the climbers' approach to the crag. A trap for foxes, these tiny pens had a cantilever plank bated with a goose hung from its tip, the fox would walk the plank, fall into the pen and starve. It proved an effective control for fell foxes. Although hunting with hounds is outlawed, this device is unlikely to be restored as sentimental walkers will attempt to set the foxes free and get bitten for their pains!

The path towards Gill Cove is intermittently pitched, more so the higher one gets; avoid the apparent worn stony gully right, keep to the solid footing. When eventually the saddle is gained, go right, north, and definitely give the notion of a cross-over pass short shrift; the marking of a path on OS maps just must be an error. Two paths head northwards, the ridge path proper deserving greater attention, for it gives the better views back, notably the fabulous view of Brim Fell which graces the cover of this book, as seen from the little rocky top of Great How Crags. **3** The path to Swirl Hause from Levers Water has grown in popularity over the years. It has its moments of wetness, though is never in doubt. Those of a fellwandering inclination might trek upstream with Swirl Hause Beck, visiting the adjacent rigg with its pools and mine. Of greatest appeal is the coarse roche moutonnee, pock-marked and banded, the variety of volcanic forms is quite interesting. The upper cove is thoroughly hemmed in by crags, miners calling it the Prison with good reason. Hence the enclosing rocky ridge rising steeply from Swirl Hause became known as the Prison Band, there is only the most modest amount of hands-on-rock work encountered during the ascent from the cairn; by and large it's fun.

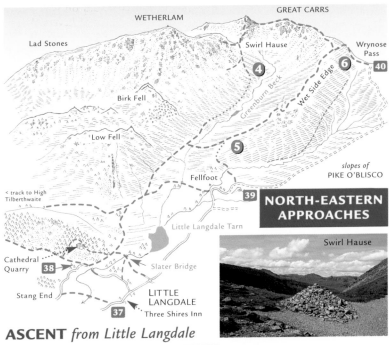

NORTH-EASTERN APPROACHES

Swirl Hause

ASCENT *from Little Langdale*

There are two prime routes out of the Brathay valley, the more direct heads up Greenburn Beck valley. **4** From the hamlet of Little Langdale begin by visiting Slater Bridge. Whatever else your day may hold in store,

The Prison Band from the approach to Swirl Hause

simply to step upon this little footbridge brings a special magic to the outdoor adventure, a work of art that has stood the test of time, a visual and tactile exhibition of the beauty of local slate. Follow the walled lane by Low and High Hall Garths, then the subsequent open track leading to the old Greenburn copper mine, the site a protected monument. Thereafter, walkers take differing lines up the valley, a feeble path only coming into existence well up the valley side, after crossing High Keld Gill, bound for Swirl Hause and the Prison Band ridge.

5 Ridge walks are always the best endeavours, and the Great Carrs ridge a classic high way. Start from Fellfoot by Bridgend and the Greenburn track crossing a footbridge after the intake wall gate, clambering onto the low ridge heading for Rough Crags and Wet Side Edge; a further approach begins from Castle How, fording the infant Brathay to step onto Hollin Crag ridge end (consult the Great Carrs chapter: page 92).

6 The first tourists were guided to the 'awful' summits on pony back, hence it's no bad idea, in fact an awfully good idea, to use whatever horse-power is at your disposal to save your legs and reduce the ascent to a mere 1,350 feet/411 metres by starting from the top of the Wrynose Pass. The one disadvantage – it does limit your choice in circular walk targets.

The Scafells overtopping Great Carrs from the summit

The Summit

A place of congregation, on a small flat plateau. Most visitors bound up on the skyline walk from Coniston, pleased to have made it to the highest point on their round – bring on the Old Man or Wetherlam. The rugged cairn, built close to the northern downfall into the depths of the Greenburn valley, providing a navigational fix and a focus for happy relaxation after the strenuous climb. The view over Wetherlam and across Great Carrs to the Scafells *(bottom left)* gives a sense of airy space to the situation; note the Isle of Man sits precisely on top of Grey Friar.

Safe Descents

The Prison Band is steep, but in all bar icy conditions is a secure line for Coniston, via Swirl Hause, turning right for Levers Water. The ridge path S leads to the Levers Hause depression, also a sound line for Coniston. The ridge N curving round by Great Carrs is without complication down via Wet Side Edge for the Wrynose Pass or into Little Langdale.

Ridge Routes to...

BRIM FELL   DESCENT *400ft*   ASCENT *370ft*   1.5 miles
Follow the broad ridge S, climbing from the depression of Levers Hause.
GREAT CARRS   DESCENT *490ft*   ASCENT *990ft*   0.3 miles
Go downhill W from the summit curving N round the rim of Broad Slack.
GREY FRIAR   DESCENT *370ft*   ASCENT *265ft*   1 mile
Descend W upon grass into the broad Fairfield saddle, joining the ridge path rising SW onto the summit plateau, passing the Matterhorn Rock.
WETHERLAM   DESCENT *620ft*   ASCENT *480ft*   1.3 miles
Take care right from the start. Descend E down the rocky Prison Band ridge, it is straightforward, but requires care in places in wet, windy or icy conditions. A large cairn marks Swirl Hause, from where the ridge path climbs easily NE, avoiding the top of Black Sails, then E to the top.

The summit cairn in early May. Notice the furtive cloud typically banking up to consume the tops

PANORAMA

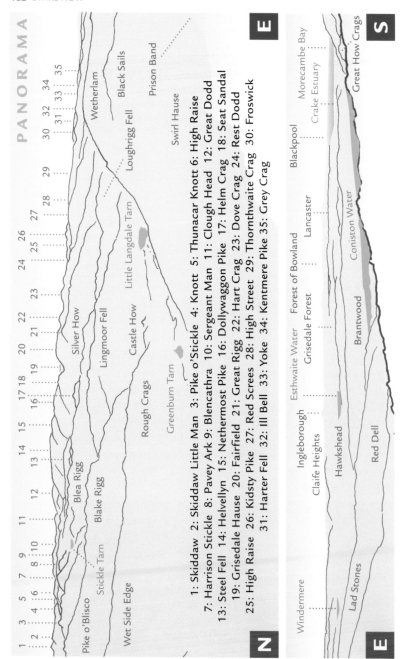

1: Skiddaw 2: Skiddaw Little Man 3: Pike o'Stickle 4: Knott 5: Thunacar Knott 6: High Raise
7: Harrison Stickle 8: Pavey Ark 9: Blencathra 10: Sergeant Man 11: Clough Head 12: Great Dodd
13: Steel Fell 14: Helvellyn 15: Nethermost Pike 16: Dollywaggon Pike 17: Helm Crag 18: Seat Sandal
19: Grisedale Hause 20: Fairfield 21: Great Rigg 22: Hart Crag 23: Dove Crag 24: Rest Dodd
25: High Raise 26: Kidsty Pike 27: Red Screes 28: High Street 29: Thornthwaite Crag 30: Froswick
31: Harter Fell 32: Ill Bell 33: Yoke 34: Kentmere Pike 35: Grey Crag

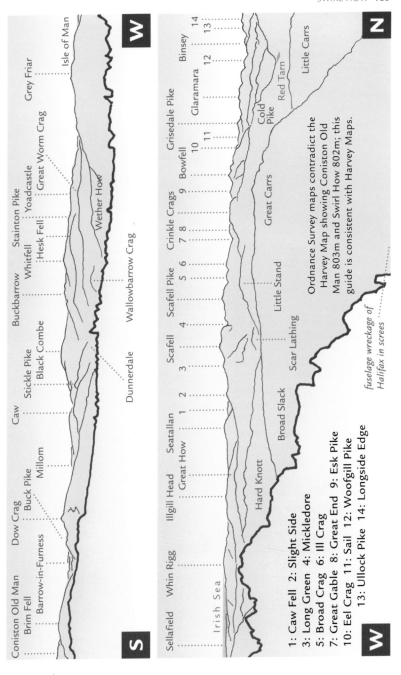

Ordnance Survey maps contradict the Harvey Map showing Coniston Old Man 803m and Swirl How 802m; this guide is consistent with Harvey Maps.

fuselage wreckage of Halifax in screes

1: Caw Fell 2: Slight Side
3: Long Green 4: Mickledore
5: Broad Crag 6: Ill Crag
7: Great Gable 8: Great End 9: Esk Pike
10: Eel Crag 11: Sail 12: Woofgill Pike
13: Ullock Pike 14: Longside Edge

WALLOWBARROW CRAG 19

Greatly appreciated by rock climbers for its sunny, and therefore quick drying, easily accessed crags; known to fellwalkers: well no, actually! In the main bypassed, accepted simply as one side of the famous gorge. This massive fist of magma, the remnant plug of a geologically ancient volcano vent, is the Duddon's focal viewpoint. During August it is draped with the most gorgeously luxuriant growth of purple heather, a delight to bees and people alike.

Access onto its rough top is confined to one narrow trod and one chink, a heather-choked gully from the bridle-path as it draws up to the low saddle on its west side.

Let's not forget the mission, to enjoy Wallowbarrow Crag. Engage in a round ramble through the gorge to Fickle Steps, ascending to Grassguards track, back along the bridle-path, only then stepping onto the crag-top, to appreciate its unique Duddon credentials.

From lower down the dale at Low Wood

GREY FRIAR

292 metres   958 feet

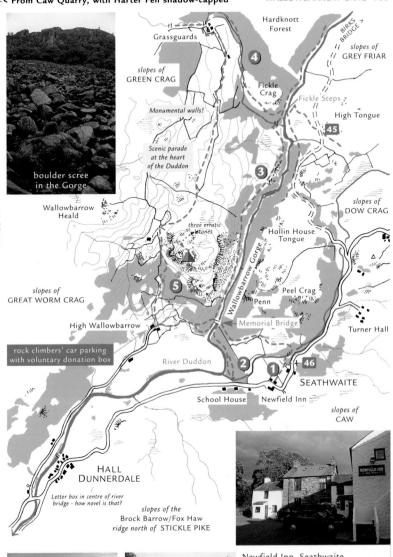

Hardknott
Forest

BIRKS
BRIDGE

Grassguards

slopes of
GREY FRIAR

slopes of
GREEN CRAG

4

Fickle
Crag

Fickle Steps

Monumental walls!

High Tongue

*Scenic parade
at the heart
of the Duddon*

45

3

boulder scree
in the Gorge

Wallowbarrow
Heald

slopes of
DOW CRAG

*three erratic
stones*

Hollin House
Tongue

slopes of
GREAT WORM CRAG

Wallowbarrow Gorge

5

Peel Crag

Penn

High Wallowbarrow

Memorial Bridge

Turner Hall

rock climbers' car parking
with voluntary donation box

River Duddon

2

1

46

SEATHWAITE

School House

Newfield Inn

slopes of
CAW

HALL
DUNNERDALE

*Letter box in centre of river
bridge - how novel is that?*

*slopes of the
Brock Barrow/Fox Haw
ridge north of STICKLE PIKE*

EXCEPTIONAL SCALE

one kilometre   one mile

Newfield Inn, Seathwaite

(left) Summit carpet of heather

(near left) The Duddon, flowing
through the Wallowbarrow Gorge,
viewed from the Memorial footbridge

ASCENT *from Seathwaite*

1 Opposite Newfield Inn a footpath leads, via gates, to a small footbridge spanning Tarn Beck. This passes a small weir, skirts a marsh, coming alongside a wall to arrives at the Memorial footbridge; the seat, up to the right, is not a clue to a secret route onto the hidden height of Penn. **2** The bridge can also be reached from a footpath that leaves the valley road opposite the old School House; again crossing a Tarn Beck footbridge, weave through woodland with the option of looking at the Duddon/Tarn Beck confluence. **3** Either head direct for High Wallowbarrow Farm by wood and meadow or, better still, venture up the gorge, right. Progress through a fantasy world of rock and native woodland via stiles: the boulder scree spilling from the high crag is particularly impressive. The path climbs, then dips to a wooden footbridge over Grassguards Gill, before advancing to Fickle Steps. **4** A path from the open common descends to cross the stepping stones (not always quite so simple, being prone to submersion). A path angles up the woodland half-left to rock steps, then via a hand-gate, following the gill to the forest track access to Grassguards; go left crossing the footbridge – a permissive path is recommended that orbits the farmhouse and buildings on the right by hand-gates. Follow the bridle-track by a short thick-walled lane and an enclosure marshalled by deer-excluding gateways. **5** From High Wallowbarrow Farm follow the bridleway left from the barn-end, ascending via gates. Climb from beneath the mighty crag, veer left to come alongside a wall. As this nears the top, either look for the weakness right, no path up a gully *(above)*, or higher, find a thin path onto the top and be exalted!

Caw from the summit

(facing page) The Duddon dale from the pike rock, east of the cairnless summit

PANORAMA

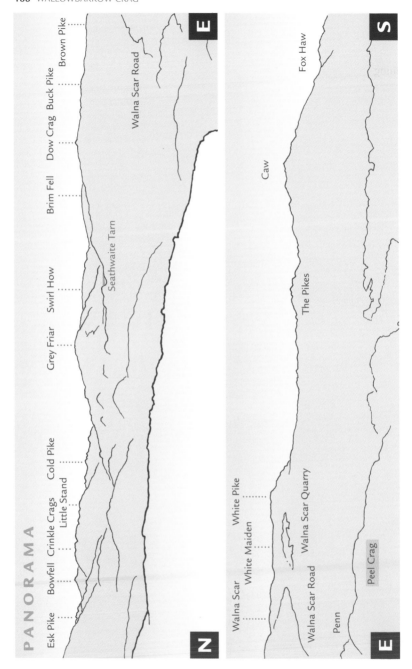

Top panorama (N to E):
Esk Pike · Bowfell · Crinkle Crags · Little Stand · Cold Pike · Grey Friar · Swirl How · Brim Fell · Dow Crag · Buck Pike · Brown Pike · Seathwaite Tarn · Walna Scar Road

Bottom panorama (E to S):
Walna Scar · White Pike · White Maiden · Walna Scar Quarry · Walna Scar Road · Penn · Peel Crag · The Pikes · Caw · Fox Haw

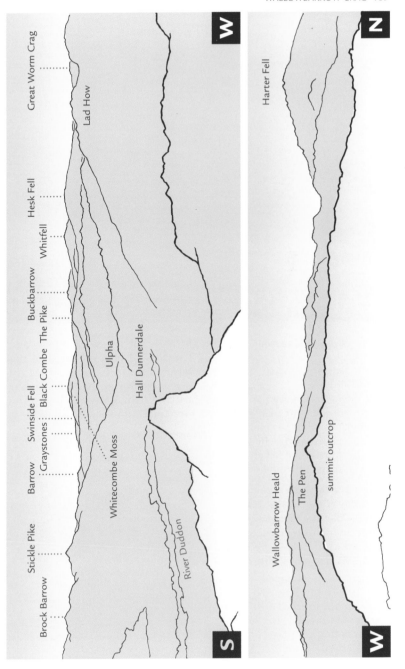

W

Great Worm Crag
Lad How
Hesk Fell
Whitfell
Buckbarrow
The Pike
Ulpha
Black Combe
Hall Dunnerdale
Swinside Fell
Barrow
Graystones
Whitecombe Moss
Stickle Pike
River Duddon
Brock Barrow

S

N

Harter Fell

Wallowbarrow Heald
The Pen
summit outcrop

W

Off to climb Walna Scar... the rough road that crosses the high pass between Coniston and Seathwaite? The age-old highway loved to this day by walkers, cyclists and motor-bikers alike *(seen below on the rise towards Brown Pike)*? No, the fell! Stand in the bar at the Newfield Inn, look down at the regular striated dark and light slate flag floor. This tells of another side of Walna Scar's more recent history, as a source for excellent building stone: the gaping quarries that line the western slope of the fell are fascinating 'scars' of another kind.

The fell effectively completes the Dow Crag ridge to the south. The highest point, a grassy hummock of a top, is bettered as a summit by both White Maiden and White Pike.

Though easily 'bagged' from the old road, the fell has excellent approaches over little trammelled country, suiting the fellwandering connoisseur.

621 *metres*   2,037 *feet*

ASCENT *from Coniston*

1 The Walna Scar Road springs from the centre of Coniston, climb on an initially steep gradient, past the old station. The toil eventually abates, thank goodness; progress is more leisurely in the country lane, rising to the fell-gate onto the common, where most car-borne walkers park and embark. A minority of 4 x 4 drivers park beyond Boo Tarn. At least they should get the message that driving over the pass is inappropriate. The track climbs through two stone cuttings, crosses Cove Bridge and mounts the steep flank of Brown Pike. The ingenious sentry box shelter gives a moment's cause to pause, prior to reaching the saddle; go left (south) onto the gentle apex of the fell.

(below) The Duddon aspect

Two views of the Walna Scar slate quarry: *(top)* the unprotected upper hollow; this deserves the utmost caution, especially in mist, and *(below)* the adjacent partitioning arete. The whole site is quite fascinating, part mined, part quarried, all the residual effects well worth seeking out, but watch your step!

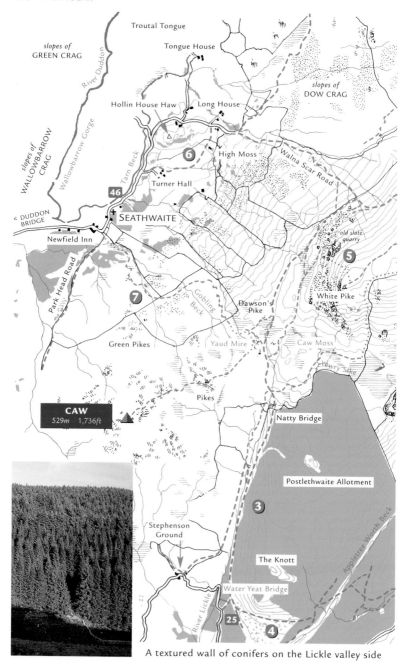

Troutal Tongue

slopes of
GREEN CRAG

Tongue House

slopes of
DOW CRAG

Hollin House Haw   Long House

High Moss

Walna Scar Road

6

Turner Hall

46

old slate
quarry

< DUDDON
BRIDGE

SEATHWAITE

5

Newfield Inn

Park Head Road

7

Gobling Beck

Dawson's
Pike

White Pike

Green Pikes

Yaud Mire

Caw Moss

Yewry Stke

CAW
529m   1,736ft

Pikes

Natty Bridge

Postlethwaite Allotment

3

Stephenson
Ground

The Knott

Appletree Worth Beck

Water Yeat Bridge

River Lickle

25

4

A textured wall of conifers on the Lickle valley side

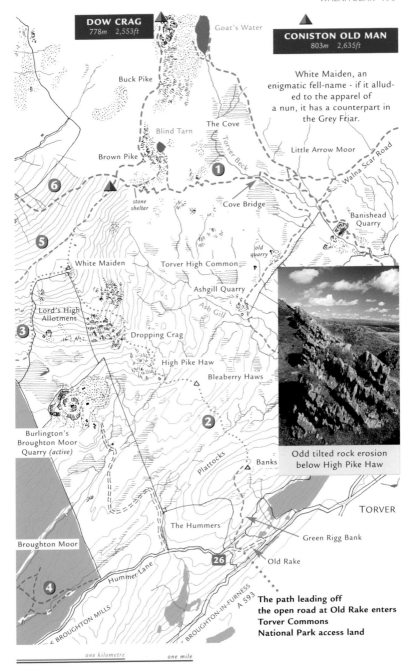

DOW CRAG
778m 2,553ft

Goat's Water

CONISTON OLD MAN
803m 2,635ft

White Maiden, an
enigmatic fell-name - if it allud-
ed to the apparel of
a nun, it has a counterpart in
the Grey Friar.

Buck Pike

Blind Tarn

The Cove

Little Arrow Moor

Brown Pike

Torver Beck

Walna Scar Road

6

1

stone
shelter

Cove Bridge

Banishead
Quarry

5

old
quarry

White Maiden

Torver High Common

Ashgill Quarry

Lord's High
Allotment

Ash Gill

3

Dropping Crag

High Pike Haw

Bleaberry Haws

Odd tilted rock erosion
below High Pike Haw

2

Burlington's
Broughton Moor
Quarry *(active)*

Plattocks

Banks

Bucks

TORVER

The Hummers

Green Rigg Bank

Broughton Moor

26

Old Rake

Hummer Lane

A 593

BROUGHTON-IN-FURNESS

BROUGHTON MILLS

4

The path leading off
the open road at Old Rake enters
Torver Commons
National Park access land

one kilometre

one mile

Buck Pike, Dow Crag and Coniston Old Man from the standard cairn on Banks

ASCENT *from Hummer Lane*

2 The small access point, off Hummer Lane above Torver, is the presage to a most enjoyable, if unconventional approach. The only path of the ascent leads via Green Rigg Bank to the handsome standard cairn *(above)*, prominently sited on the eastern shoulder of Banks, a Torver village landmark. Cross over the grassy ridge, north westward, descend into the curiously named damp hollow of Plattocks. Thread a way up through the impending bracken, an old wall a guide by a small quarry to the cairn surmounting Bleaberry Haws. Slip through the next narrow valley depression with its small quarry ruin, to embark on the real climb of the day; but first seek out the oddly eroded, steeply pitched, bedrock *(see previous page)*, while clambering over or round High Pike Haw. Pass up by a marshy hollow to a sheepfold tucked under Dropping Crag; note the subterranean gill in the boulders above. Step on the broad ridge through the outcropping to join the rising wall to White Maiden.

ASCENT *from the Lickle valley*

3 The perfect approach with Walna Scar experienced as a valley-head mountain. Reversed, this route may also be woven into a circular expedition, using the well-marked bridleway, through the Broughton Moor forest **4** as the means of getting back to the Hummer Lane start of route **2**. Either follow the forest track direct from the recessed gate at GR238928, advancing

to the stile and wooden footbridge through the ravine at Natty Bridge. Alternatively, after expending the extra effort of crossing Water Yeat Bridge and following the minor road up to Stephenson Ground, one may follow the gated bridle-path up the western side of the Lickle Gorge *(page 194)* a lovely approach focused on White Pike. Where this in effect crosses the continuing footpath from Natty Bridge, go forward (east) following the grooved path weaving onto Caw Moss, crossing a small flag bridge *(see page 196)* with White Pike dominant. The occasional wanderer keeps the path discernible as it leads on towards a gateway in a wall - with a tarn beyond. Ignore, take off up the fellside, keeping this wall close right. This is a simple pathless means of getting onto White Maiden... *and a safe escape route off the ridge in bad weather too*.

5 The Walna Scar Road is the natural destination of the Lickle head path, via the base of the spoil banks of Walna Scar Quarry. As the bridleway reaches the brow you encounter a fork. Neither path has a mastery of marshy ground, use by bikers to the detrimental effect of the surface in places. The more commonly followed footpath leads straight on by Dawson's Pike, comes under the slate spoil, and follows the intake wall direct to the Road. The right-hand bridle-path makes a better fist of getting up among the quarry workings, so is the preferred option. The vast quantity of slate tip suggests a major hollowing of the fell and, sure enough, such is found. If lured into the main quarry, know the only way out is the way you went in! Keep up the right-hand side of the workings to get the most stupendous, nay fearful, view into the cavity. One cannot look upon such scenes without being aware of what it represents in human toil. This is old labour before the unions! The fellside above is without incident; on reaching the plateau top slant right to visit the cairn on White Pike, a viewpoint par excellence down the Lickle valley to the sea.

6 Walkers from the Duddon side can use Walna Scar as a short day option, useful if the cloud base rules out any chance of a view from Dow Crag. The Walna Scar Road branches from the valley road half a mile north of the Newfield Inn, above Seathwaite Bridge. Becoming a rough track after a gate, it climbs to a further gate with slate tip close at hand. Centuries of wear, added to by modern traffic, motor-bikes in particular, compound natural surface damage. **7** An off-road route can be followed almost directly from the Newfield Inn. Embark upon the Park Head Road, bearing left up the old drove-way *(consult page 70)*. From the hurdle gate at the top, cross Yaud Mire, pass Dawson's Pike by the large quartz outcrop linking up with route **5**, leading by Walna Scar quarry.

A massive retaining wall of slates

White Pike from the old quarryman's path traversing Caw Moss

The Summit

An apology for a cairn marks the top of a grassy pillow rise, the view is excellent, though constricted by Brown Pike to the north. You'll tick this one off and speed on to rocky White Maiden *(above)*, then the prow end of the ridge at White Pike, for the best fell-top sensations.

Safe Descents

The Walna Scar Road is the obvious option E or W. Should you be tempted to descend off White Pike, watch out for crags but, more specifically, if you head NW towards the slate quarries, an ability to fly will be your only salvation from the unprotected edge.

Ridge Routes to...

The Scafells from the summit

CAW   2.5 miles

DESCENT *280ft*   ASCENT *190ft*

Follow the wall off White Maiden, traverse Caw Moss heading SW onto the ridge via the Pike.

DOW CRAG   1 mile

DESCENT *72 ft*   ASCENT *585 ft*

Go N over the Walna Scar pass, climbing via cairns on Brown and Buck Pikes. Follow the exciting edge to the culminating cliff-top summit battlement – holding on to your hat in a gale will be the least of your concerns!

PANORAMA from White Maiden

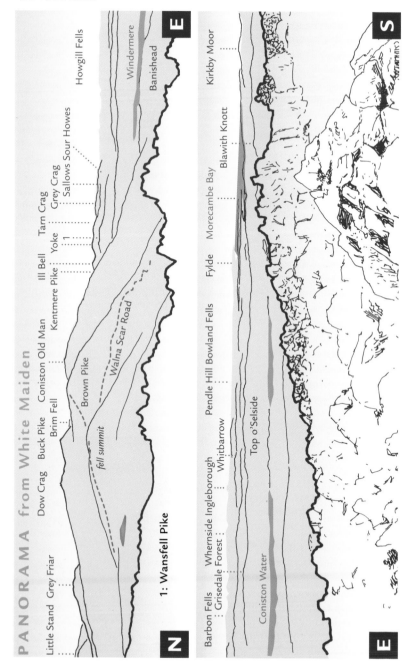

Little Stand Grey Friar Dow Crag Buck Pike Coniston Old Man Kentmere Pike Ill Bell Yoke Tarn Crag Grey Crag Sallows Sour Howes Howgill Fells

Brim Fell

Brown Pike

Walna Scar Road

fell summit

Windermere

Banishead

E

N

1: Wansfell Pike

Barbon Fells Grisedale Forest Whernside Ingleborough Pendle Hill Bowland Fells Fylde Morecambe Bay Blawith Knott Kirkby Moor

Whitbarrow

Top o'Selside

Coniston Water

S

E

W

Yoadcastle

Hesk Fell
Stainton Pike

Burn Moor
Whitfell

The Pike
White Pike

Buckbarrow
Caw
Stoneside Hill
Great Stickle
Stickle Pike

Whitecombe Moss
Black Combe

Graystones
Swinside Fell

Barrow-in-Furness
Duddon Estuary
Millom

Grisebeck

S

N

Esk Pike
13
14
12
11
10
Scafell Pike
9
8
Hard Knott
7
6
Pillar
5
4
Haycock
3
2
Caw Fell
1
Harter Fell

Illgill Head

Green Crag
Whin Rigg
Crook Crag

Woodend Height
Muncaster Fell
Great Worm Crag
Sellafield

W

1: Great How 2: Yewbarrow 3: Red Pike 4: Scoat Fell 5: Slight Side 6: Scafell 7: Mickledore 8: Broad Crag
9: Ill Crag 10: Great End 11: Esk Hause 12: Bowfell 13: Crinkle Crags/Long Top 14: Little Stand

WETHERLAM

21

Frequently, glances to the southern quarter of Lakeland fall upon Wetherlam, a prominent marker for the Coniston Fells. Whether first viewed from across Windermere or, most strikingly, from Elterwater Common on the Red Bank road near High Close *(below)*, the fell exhibits an elegant mass. Wetherlam is one of the most complex mountains in the district, not so much in terms of surface features, but rather in its hidden depths – its 'holey-ness'. For all one may eulogise about one fell or another, Wetherlam has the greatest array of route choices of any among the Southern Fells. Boldly individual, few can reach this summit on a decent day and harbour any sense of disappointment. There is more than bulky form, for down the centuries its wealth of copper and dense fine-grained slate has attracted the attention of industrious man. Deep shafts, levels and open quarries

762 *metres*   2,500 *feet*

Wetherlam Edge from Hawk Rigg

Wetherlam and Levers Water from the gully at the top of Raven Tor on Brim Fell

The fell-name appears to mean 'wether loam', source of a coloured soil used for identifying wethers, young male sheep not to be kept for tupping

The stance for the view above is a personal favourite location in the Coniston Fells, a viewpoint I have returned to on numerous occasions

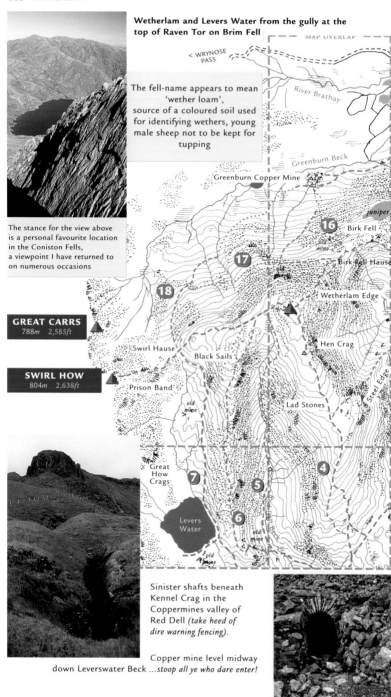

MAP OVERLAP

< WRYNOSE PASS

River Brathay

Greenburn Beck

Greenburn Copper Mine

juniper

16 Birk Fell

old mine

17

Birk Fell Hause

18

Wetherlam Edge

GREAT CARRS
788m   2,585ft

Swirl Hause

Hen Crag

Black Sails

SWIRL HOW
804m   2,638ft

Prison Band

old mine

Lad Stones

Steel Edge

Great How Crags

7

4

5

6

Levers Water

old mine

old mine

Sinister shafts beneath Kennel Crag in the Coppermines valley of Red Dell (take heed of dire warning fencing).

Copper mine level midway down Leverswater Beck ...stoop all ye who dare enter!

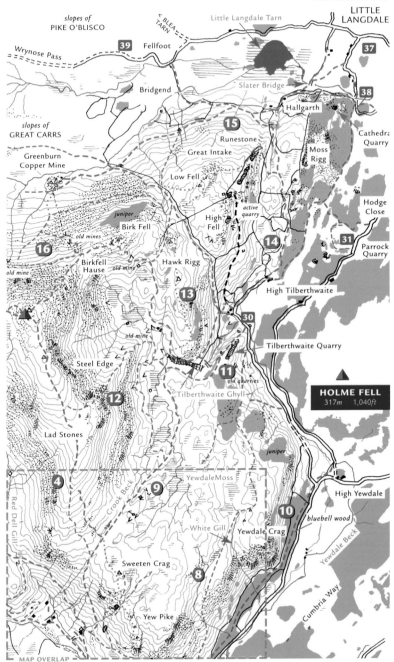

slopes of
PIKE O'BLISCO

BLEA TARN

Little Langdale Tarn

LITTLE
LANGDALE

Wrynose Pass

39 Fellfoot

37

Bridgend

Slater Bridge

38

slopes of
GREAT CARRS

Hallgarth

15

Cathedral
Quarry

Greenburn
Copper Mine

Runestone

Great Intake

Moss
Rigg

Low Fell

juniper

active
quarry

Hodge
Close

Birk Fell

High
Fell

old mines

14

31

16

Parrock
Quarry

Birkfell
Hause

Hawk Rigg

old mine

old mine

High Tilberthwaite

13

old mine

30

Tilberthwaite Quarry

Steel Edge

12

11

old quarries

▲ **HOLME FELL**
317m   1,040ft

Tilberthwaite Ghyll

Lad Stones

juniper

YewdaleMoss

4

9

White Gill

High Yewdale

10

bluebell wood

Sweeten Crag

Yewdale Crag

8

Yew Pike

Cumbria Way

Yewdale Beck

Red Dell Gill

Crook Beck

MAP OVERLAP

penetrate into its colourful interior, none of which can be considered safe for the average inquisitive fell wanderer. The location of these cavities is a surface quest. Those mines with easiest access have gained tight plain fencing to prevent calamity. Of recent decades several incautious folk have come a fatal cropper – *let none be Fellranger readers!*

The four aspects of Wetherlam are quite distinct. The northern slopes, tumbling as crags and scree into the Greenburn valley, are steep and austere: the tenacious endeavour of copper miners to win their ore on this flank is quite breathtaking. These waters feeding the Brathay flow into Windermere. The eastern slopes, initially no less dauntingly steep, are given extra spice by the imposition of Tilberthwaite Ghyll. The upper ravine, draped alpine-fashion in larch and flanked by slate quarries, leads up into shallow coves with the undulating indefinite alp of the Yewdale Fells to its south. Irregular shapely ridges run from its north down by Low Fell towards Slater Bridge in Little Langdale. The southern perspective is dominated by two great ridges. The Yewdale Fells form the first craggy rebuff from the village of Coniston, but above this the Lad Stones ridge rises imperiously to the summit. Immediately west of this lies the wild recess of Red Dell and Black Sails' strangely neglected ridge. From Swirl How, the pivotal summit on the main ridge, the Prison Band ridge, leads east to a curious saddle, Swirl Hause, the simple umbilical connection with Wetherlam.

Not the highest, but so placed as to feature in the plans of many grand horseshoe walk itineraries. In the normal course of events Coniston Old Man will be the initial prize, once upon the ridge, Brim Fell and Swirl How quickly succumb. While a few walkers will descend Prison Band and be tempted to sidle down to Levers Water, the inclusion of Wetherlam gives the outing a real flourish.

(above) Little Langdale from Cathedral quarry

(left) Gorse in full bloom on Yewdale Pike from Far End meadows in Coniston

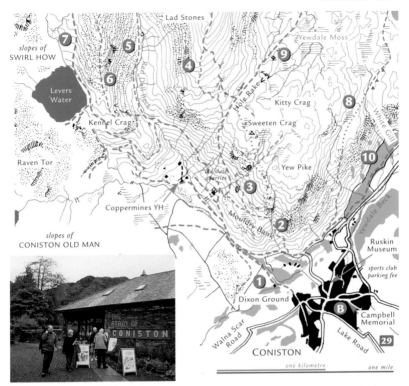

First port of call for anyone wishing to get the best grounding on the Coniston area is the Ruskin Museum, the old railway signboard a reminder of the beginnings of popular tourism to the area. (below) The heart of the Coppermines valley centred about the youth hostel, the former mine office; see copper works spoil tailings and, top left, the Burlington slate quarry still actively worked.

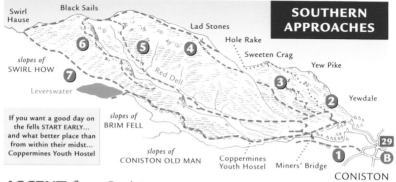

SOUTHERN APPROACHES

Swirl Hause • Black Sails • Lad Stones • Hole Rake • Sweeten Crag • Yew Pike • slopes of SWIRL HOW • Red Dell • Leverswater • Yewdale

If you want a good day on the fells START EARLY... and what better place than from within their midst... Coppermines Youth Hostel

slopes of BRIM FELL • slopes of CONISTON OLD MAN • Coppermines Youth Hostel • Miners' Bridge • CONISTON

ASCENT *from Coniston*

Aspirations normally focus on gaining the high Lad Stones ridge, the natural start/finish to the perennially popular Coniston skyline walk embracing Swirl How, Brim Fell and Coniston Old Man. There are three lead-in routes to the Hole Rake gap, where the ridge effectively begins. **1** Above the Sun Hotel follow the path from Dixon Ground, which leads to and across Miners' Bridge. Go left on the main valley track; as it levels, fork right on the old quarry track. Be sure to take the third left turn in a zag-zag course, on an incline path to Hole Rake. **2** Follow the road access into the Coppermines valley from beside the Black Bull which becomes a rough track; beyond the grid branch off up the Mouldry Bank slope, contouring from an old cairn under Rascal How to link with route **1**. Or **3**, bear up the old quarry path, right, taking care where the quarry has collapsed and removed a chunk of the track. This route winds up through the upper portion of the Blue Quarry onto the fell above; either climb over Sweeten Crag or find the green path leading northwest by Kitty Crag to Hole Rake. The undulating rough fell alp from Yew Pike to Yewdale Crag has its high point on Sweeten Crag, an absorbing place to wander at ease with the world – if relieved of the impetus or burden to get to the top of Wetherlam.

9 The path that leads through Hole Rake aims down to Tilberthwaite Ghyll by minor slate sites. However, this is no immediate help when Wetherlam needs to be climbed. **4** Two paths have developed to the Lad Stones ridge. One starts short of the top of the pass, dipping through the gill, weaving onto the ridge-end. While a more cautious path departs over stepping stones before the rushy tarn north of the rake, mounting assuredly onto the ridge northwestward through early slabs, turning at a large block of bedrock. On the ridge-top the two paths join, then proceed to the summit. Somehow it seems to take far longer than expected, via two pronounced steps in the ridge.

5 From the first turn above the quarryman's terrace, known as Irish Row, a path leads towards Red Dell. This is copper mines country sure

enough, for above the cascading Red Dell Beck are leats and water-wheel pits. The Thriddle incline, pitches up the north side of Kennel Crags with evidence of long abandoned deep workings into the Bonsor vein. Bracken fronds grow around their gaping mouths like lures to a death trap - a landscape full of interest and considerable danger! A path leads on, past the site of a 17th-century copper ore grinding mill, into the Red Dell valley. Pass a large erratic, then a sheepfold before fording the gill. At its head, climb on the east side; a faint trod guides up to cairns leading to the peaty hollow, just to the west of the summit.

6 The neglected Black Sails ridge provides a gem of an ascent. Climb the Thriddle incline, pass a mine level halfway with two gate-grilled levels at the top. Go left to the saddle, follow naturally right up the ridge, with faint evidence of a path; One may also join the ridge from the outflow of Levers Water. Look out for the narrow banded rocks *(above)* from where there is a superb view back over Levers Water to Raven Tor and the Old Man. The path tends to avoid the ridge-top, though for no good reason; notice the intensity of lichen growth. At the top the ridge constricts to give a fine view back down Red Dell. One may clamber up to the cairn on Black Sails *(right)*, or slant half-right to join the main ridge path, from Swirl Hause, to reach the summit.

7 The steady route, suitable when poor conditions dictate a less exposed line or for easy descent, continues up the Swirl Hause Beck valley from the outflow of Levers Water. Marshy ground is the only hazard to the saddle's cairn. Note, this is more a T-junction, the path into the Greenburn Beck valley ahead, a minor trod by comparison with the worn trail at your feet. Go right (east), traversing the north slope of Black Sails to reach the summit; consistently enjoy the fabulous views to the north.

Two paths from Coniston form interesting approaches to Tilberthwaite, extending the exploration of Wetherlam's eastern foothills. **8** Pass by Holly How Youth Hostel, turning up a path by Far End Cottages to join a lateral path from the Coppermines valley access track as it becomes a rough track. Go through the hand-gate, follow a path climbing directly opposite. The climb is nowhere near as tough as you might think and has

Low Tilberthwaite, with spinning gallery/wool store
Footbridge in Tilberthwaite Ghyll

the most marvellous outlook; small cairns help identify the route. Cross the headstream of White Gill (which is a striking water-slide feature from Yewdale), perhaps visiting the Yewdale Crag headland, before weaving down through juniper and Penny Rigg slate quarry/mine effects to the Tilberthwaite road. **10** Alternatively, a gentle path threads through the woodland at the foot of the Yewdale Crag scarp. Fording White Gill you may notice right, close to the road, a 19th-century lime kiln, which exploited the narrow band of mountain limestone in this vicinity for pasture-improving quick lime. In season the continuing path is renowned for its deep-pile carpet of bluebells.

ASCENT *from Low Tilberthwaite and Little Langdale*

Enquire of any fellwalker how many ways there are to the top of Wetherlam, you may get the answer of no more than four. But once you start looking a plethora of options emerges, particularly from the east and north. **11** Paths ascend either side of Tilberthwaite Ghyll, with through connection mid-course via a scenic footbridge. The linear slate quarry on the south side deserves a brief internal inspection. **12** Enter an area of really old copper mines at the upper end of the ghyll ravine. Cross the footbridge, go right, then left, onto the base of the Steel Edge ridge. Starting as a grassy rigg, it narrows impressively to culminate in a spot of hands-on scrambling, of the easiest kind, up to the Lad Stones ridge-top,

near a perfect horseshoe-shaped pool. A word of warning: if you choose to descend by this ridge, do not be lured into the gully on the north side. This looks to be the way but most definitely is not. Its loose angular scree is horrid. **13** From the point the main path on the north

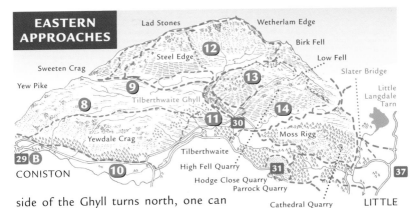

EASTERN APPROACHES

Lad Stones
Wetherlam Edge
Birk Fell
Steel Edge
12
Low Fell
Sweeten Crag
Slater Bridge
Yew Pike
13
Little Langdale Tarn
9
Tilberthwaite Ghyll
8
14
11 **30**
Moss Rigg
Yewdale Crag
Tilberthwaite
29 **B**
High Fell Quarry
31
37
CONISTON
10
Hodge Close Quarry
Parrock Quarry
Cathedral Quarry
LITTLE LANGDALE
Ruestone quarry

side of the Ghyll turns north, one can step onto the low ridge, right, no path, hold to the skyline via the little cairned knolltops of Hawk Rigg *(page 208)*, then easily reconnect with the continuing path from the head of Tilberthwaite Ghyll. This leads round two shallow combes of Dry Cove with further evidence of old copper mines. By new pitching, step onto Birk Fell; off to the right find a cairn indicating a lovely view. From Birkfell Hause the high prow of Wetherlam Edge looms. The climb includes several rocky steps, but nothing extraordinary; the erosion suggesting that the repair work needs to continue.

Little Langdale Tarn from Low Fell

14 From High Tilberthwaite two tracks proceed north. Take the left-hand option. Copper and slate were once ferried along here by pack-mules from Little Langdale. The track begins to descend; an old quarry track forks left; follow this up to the ridge-end slate tip via a gate. Climb to the mid-point of Runestone quarry, the name indicates naturally inscribed slate with a runic-look. Branch right and climb pathless to the summit of Low Fell. Low Fell has a wonderful carpet of bilberries and an excellent viewpoint over Little Langdale *(page 209)* through the Blea Tarn gap to the Langdale Pikes (*an elevated version of the scene on page 212*). It's a hilltop to spend idle time on. A spidery path leads west from the summit, descending Great Intake to a ladder-stile. Find a path linking over a small saddle, north of Hawk Rigg, down to the popular path. Go right to climb onto Birk Fell.

15 Wetherlam dominates Little Langdale *(see below)*, the climb is irresistible. From the Three Shires Inn make for Slater Bridge *(above)*. Among the trees above is Cathedral or Little Langdale quarry, well worth seeking out; be careful should you make entry via the tunnel, heed signs.

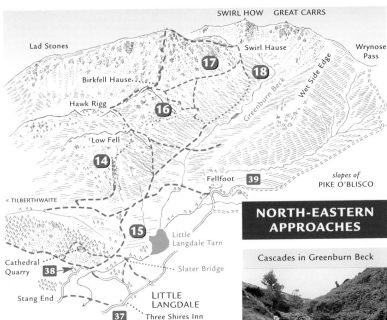

SWIRL HOW   GREAT CARRS

Lad Stones

Swirl Hause

Wrynose Pass

Birkfell Hause

17

18

Hawk Rigg

16

Greenburn Beck

Wet Side Edge

Low Fell

14

Fellfoot **39**

slopes of
PIKE O'BLISCO

< TILBERTHWAITE

15

Little Langdale Tarn

Cathedral Quarry **38**

Slater Bridge

Stang End

LITTLE LANGDALE

37 Three Shires Inn

NORTH-EASTERN APPROACHES

Cascades in Greenburn Beck

Pass along the narrow lane by Low and High Hallgarths, pursuing the subsequent track. The old road from Tilber-thwaite joins acutely, from the left. The track forks, go left. This rises with a wall to the right, pause and take a good look north over Bridgend to the Langdale Pikes *(page 212)*. As the wall drifts away, a narrow path can be followed left up the bracken slope of Great Intake to a

ladder-stile bound for the saddle next to Hawk Rigg. Or conti nue through the intake wall gate, then veer up left. However, the main attraction can be more simply gained by staying with the valley track along Greenburn Beck *(above)*, rising to the old Greenburn Copper Mine *(left)* – a protected monument, inspect respectfully.

Dependent on the mountain's mood, Wetherlam hangs either impressively or dauntingly above this industrious scene. While many walkers blithely stride on up the valley, giving only the briefest thought to the old workings, there is every good reason to take a more thorough inspection, seeking out the associated remains

at higher 'levels'. The whole mining and quarrying history of the fell arrants an exclusive walking guide for the inquisitive surface explorer – *practical itineraries by local mine expert Eric Holland can be found in his field guide published by Cicerone Press.*

16 Once free of the ruins, angle half-left finding a gap in the bracken, seek an obviously engineered miners' path slanting left up the steep fell-side. An early cairn indicates a branch path leading half-right up to the Long Crag Level; the main grass path climbs to Pave York Levels, three mine adits, one above the other. Traces of the rail incline remain by which the ore was conveyed to the crushing mill and dressing floor below *(the bottom of this incline, the central feature in the picture on the previous page).* Weave up the fell, glancing at each dark dank level in turn, the top one probably the more intriguing *(pictured above)*. A fellwalker's path continues above, rising to Birkfell Hause, then onto the popular path climbing Wetherlam Edge. **17** Alternatively, a cairned miners' trod contours to Long Crag Level, diminishing to a sheep trod across rough slopes to Swirl Hause. **18** The more usual practice is to continue up the dale from Greenburn mine, bear half-left from the reservoir dam. Go up the fellside; there is only evidence of a path once Low and High Keld Gills have been forded. Climb the dry slope beneath any hint of scree to the Hause.

The Summit

The highest ground is a gentle dome with small rocky protuberances, the unruly summit cairn itself taking advantage of one low plinth. The site deserves a far more elegant pile – send up the man who created the Low Tilberthwaite fold and see what he can do! Certainly it's a place to consider a wide Lakeland landscape, the deep furrow of Greenburn ensuring an uninhibited prospect. In terms of traditional measure the height of the fell has a certain fulfiling neatness, 2,500 feet; metric height does no favours to British hills, they are not so large as to be a feat to scale. By feet they are climbed in a couple of hours, so let them be measured in striding feet.

Safe Descents

The ground falls innocently away to the W and S but matters to N and E give cause for stern attention. The rocky steps of Wetherlam Edge faces into a biting winter gale, but is otherwise none too troublesome. The easier routes are S down the Lad Stones ridge and W to Swirl Hause.

Ridge Route to...

SWIRL HOW   DESCENT 466 ft   ASCENT 604 ft   1.25 miles

Head W down an early stony slope, two paths converge to cross peaty ground on the shallow plateau hollow at the head of Red Dell. The clear stony path drifts across the northern flank of Black Sails before descending more steeply to Swirl Hause (at 2,033ft), clearly identified by its large cairn. The Prison Band ridge looks tough but is meekly beaten by a series of mock towers; note one particularly strikingly banded specimen a third of the way up.

Swirl How and Great Carrs from the summit

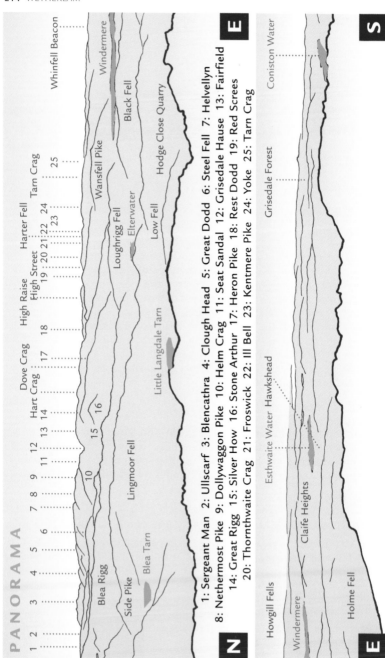

PANORAMA

1: Sergeant Man 2: Ullscarf 3: Blencathra 4: Clough Head 5: Great Dodd 6: Steel Fell 7: Helvellyn
8: Nethermost Pike 9: Dollywaggon Pike 10: Helm Crag 11: Seat Sandal 12: Griesdale Hause 13: Fairfield
14: Great Rigg 15: Silver How 16: Stone Arthur 17: Heron Pike 18: Rest Dodd 19: Red Screes
20: Thornthwaite Crag 21: Froswick 22: Ill Bell 23: Kentmere Pike 24: Yoke 25: Tarn Crag

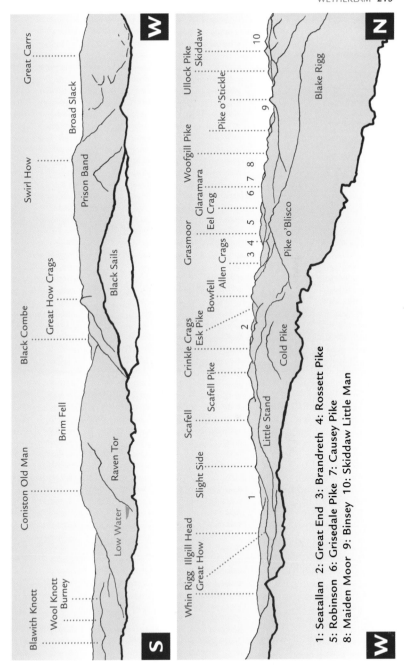

W

S

Great Carrs
Swirl How
Black Combe
Coniston Old Man
Blawith Knott

Broad Slack
Prison Band
Great How Crags
Brim Fell
Wool Knott
Burney

Black Sails
Raven Tor
Low Water

N

W

Ullock Pike · Skiddaw
Woofgill Pike
Grasmoor
Crinkle Crags
Scafell
Whin Rigg Illgill Head
Slight Side

Pike o'Stickle
Glaramara
Eel Crag
Esk Pike
Bowfell
Allen Crags
Scafell Pike
Little Stand
Great How

Blake Rigg
Pike o'Blisco
Cold Pike

10
9
8
7
6
5
4
3
2
1

1: Seatallan 2: Great End 3: Brandreth 4: Rossett Pike
5: Robinson 6: Grisedale Pike 7: Causey Pike
8: Maiden Moor 9: Binsey 10: Skiddaw Little Man

WHITFELL

22

The southwest-running rippling ridge, springing from Harter Fell and terminating upon Black Combe, is focused upon this hill, a rounded sleek-lined sentinel, keeping guard over an ancient bridle-pass: the natural target for a fell-climb or a long ridge traverse. The kind of summit that walkers find engaging, a stout cairn built upon an archaic gather of stones, whose cultural significance has long been lost. The feminine elegance of the main fell contrasts with the chunky mass of Burn Moor tagged on to its west, a Te Kanawa and Pavarotti double-act.

ASCENT *from Bigert Mire*

To the east the fell is drained by three becks, Holehouse, Tongue and Logan, the latter crossed by the access road from the Corneyfell Road, where an old coach road branches right, over Ulpha Park, by the ruins of Frith Hall, a place with a colourful history. The access road slips through the attractive environs of Logan Beck Farm *(see page 219)*, seeking a suitable parking spot betweenr Long Garth and Old Hall, with its ruined peel serving as a grandiose sheep pen. From this Duddon side there is but one approach. **1** A bridleway traverses the ridge from Bigert Mire. If the name

573 *metres*   1,880 *feet*

From Stainton Pike

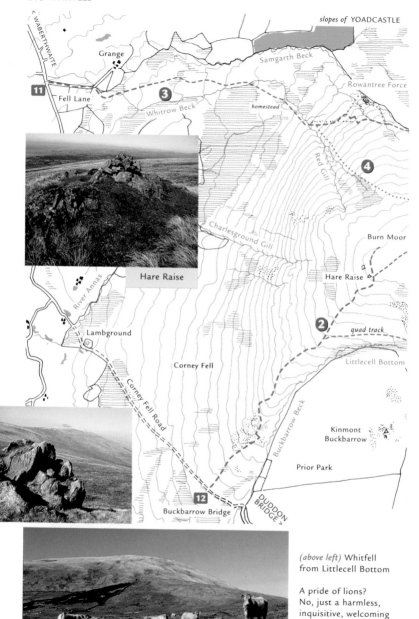

slopes of YOADCASTLE

Samgarth Beck

Rowantree Force

WABERTHWAITE

Grange

11

Fell Lane

3

Whitrow Beck

homestead

Red Gill

4

Charlesground Gill

Burn Moor

Hare Raise

Hare Raise

River Annas

Lambground

2

quad track

Littlecell Bottom

Corney Fell

Corney Fell Road

Buckbarrow Beck

Kinmont Buckbarrow

Prior Park

12

Buckbarrow Bridge

DUDDON BRIDGE

(above left) Whitfell from Littlecell Bottom

A pride of lions?
No, just a harmless, inquisitive, welcoming party of Limousin suckler cattle, on the bridleway above Bigert Mire.

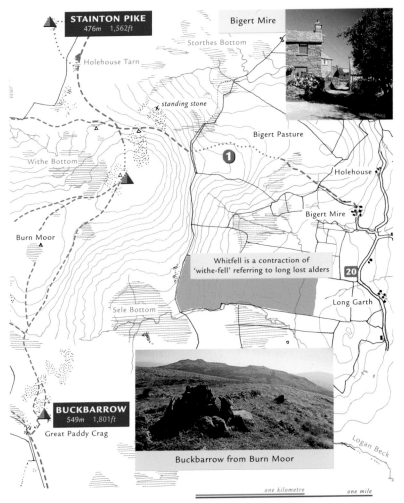

STAINTON PIKE
476m   1,562ft

Holehouse Tarn

Bigert Mire

Storthes Bottom

standing stone

Bigert Pasture

1

Withe Bottom

Holehouse

Burn Moor

Bigert Mire

20

Whitfell is a contraction of
'withe-fell' referring to long lost alders

Long Garth

Sele Bottom

BUCKBARROW
549m   1,801ft
Great Paddy Crag

Logan Beck

Buckbarrow from Burn Moor

one kilometre   one mile

Logan Beck
(*pronounced*
'log-on') on the
approach from
Corneyfell Road
to Bigert Mire

is derived from a misspelling of 'bigot', then the successors of the obstinate devotee have made a very tidy community with six cottages huddling together where once just one farm stood. There is space for one parked car at a pinch. Walk through to the gate, and bear up left on the bridle-track, passing a lone standing barn - conceivably another conversion. The track enters Bigertmire Pasture at a gate and begins purposefully enough, a tractor track used to carry feed to livestock, but this ends and the line of the bridleway fades in rising up the great pasture. Stride up to a kissing-gate in the fence, strengthening the broken intake wall. With the old path restored underfoot, rise to the a cairn at the top of the pass, bear left, now with the ridge path to the summit tumulus.

ASCENT *from Buckbarrow Bridge & Broad Oak*

2 From the Corneyfell Road at GR 132904 a bridle-track climbs to the cairn on Hare Raise, then apparently stops - the reason: it was an old peat-cutters' sled-gate. However, the table-top has no impediment to a simple traverse other than tough grass *(below)*; visit the prominent cairn en route *(see 227)*.

3 The Fell Lane approach, described in the Stainton Pike chapter *(page 160)* is the western limb of the bridleway from Bigert Mire. Follow this up Whitrow Beck as far as the gullied foot of Red Gill. Either ascend the left-hand edge of this deeply gullied forked gill onto Burn Moor. Sheep trods give some assistance to the saddle, where a small exposure of peat, the proverbial Peakland 'grough', is passed onto easier ground leading to the summit. 4 Or take the bridle-path, an engineered green-way, climbing the steeper ground eastward. Why not visit Rowantree Force just off route? The path is lost as the ground levels in the broad basin of Withe Bottom, but restored in rising to the small cairn at the highest point of the pass; then joining the crossing ridge path, climb right (south) to the top.

Purple-moor grass singeing Burn Moor, looking east to Whitfell

The Summit

Rising to a gentle dome the fell culminates upon an ancient cairn. This is a low round pile of rocks some eighteen strides wide upon which has been built a rustic, yet quite noble cairn. Inevitably, visitors have further adapted the handy stones to fashion a wind shelter, tucked in on the leeward side. Sandwiches consumed, gaze east and south into the Duddon and its spreading estuary. An old Ordnance Survey pillar *(above)* stands forlornly on a flat patch of ground to the NE.

Ridge Route to...

BUCKBARROW   DESCENT 315*ft*   ASCENT 236*ft*   1.4 miles

A path descends SW *(below)*, traversing the E slopes of Burn Moor; cross the marshy edge of Little Sell Bottom S, onto the emerging rocky edge.

STAINTON PIKE   DESCENT 250*ft*   ASCENT 20*ft*   1 mile

Descend N, a path materialises in crossing the old bridle-pass (now NW) onto the low ridge. Branch half-left to cross the plain fence before Holehouse Tarn; a narrow trod leads to the summit knoll.

PANORAMA

N

E

1 2 3 4 5 6 7 8 9 10 11 12 13 14 15 16 17 18 19 20 21 22 23 24 25 26 27 28 29 30 31

Howgill Fells
Caw · Stickle Pike
Fox Haw

The Pike

Brim Fell

Great Worm Crag · Wallowbarrow Crag

Hesk Fell

Great How
Gate Crag

(Boat How) Eskdale Moor

1: Scoat Fell 2: Red Pike 3: Pillar 4: Illgill Head 5: Robinson 6: Kirk Fell 7: Great Gable
8: Scafell 9: Scafell Pike 10: Slight Side 11: Ill Crag 12: Esk Hause 13: Esk Pike 14: Bowfell
15: Crinkle Crags 16: Green Crag 17: Little Stand 18: Harter Fell 19: Helvellyn 20: Cold Pike
21: Fairfield 22: Hart Crag 23: Dove Crag 24: Grey Friar 25: Great Carrs 26: Swirl How
27: Dow Crag 28: Coniston Old Man 29: Brown Pike 30: Walna Scar 31: White Pike

S

E

Swinside Fell

Barrow-in-Furness
Knott Hill

Dalton
Askam

Duddon Estuary

Plough Fell

Kirkby Moor Wind Cluster

Forest of Bowland
Ward's Stone

Penn

Barrow

Logan Beck

Whernside
Ingleborough

Blawith Knott

Great Stickle

At your feet an accumulation of stones, the remains of an ancient cairn, possibly an elevated Bronze Age burial site

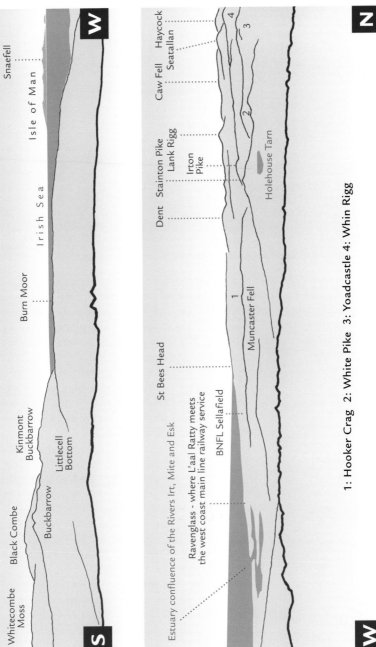

W

Snaefell

Isle of Man

Irish Sea

Burn Moor

Kinmont
Buckbarrow

Black Combe

Littlecell
Bottom

Buckbarrow

Whitecombe
Moss

S

N

Caw Fell Haycock
Seatallan

Dent Stainton Pike
Lank Rigg

Irton
Pike

Holehouse Tarn

St Bees Head

Ravenglass – where L'aal Ratty meets
the west coast main line railway service

BNFL Sellafield

Estuary confluence of the Rivers Irt, Mite and Esk

Muncaster Fell

4
3
2
1

W

1: Hooker Crag 2: White Pike 3: Yoadcastle 4: Whin Rigg

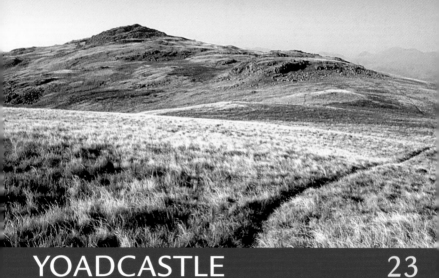

Motorists, with an eye for a scenic drive, scan their atlases and quickly home in upon the Birkerfell Road, delighting in the moorland traverse between Eskdale Green and Ulpha, the thrilling backdrop of the Scafells in grand perspective. On a good day it can be hard to keep driving, frequent lay-bys tempting one to pull in to gaze with admiration at the Lakeland alps. Those that park up and wander to the lonely shores of Devoke Water *(below)* find serenity and solace in the timeless wilderness setting. Devoke Water reflects a blue sky as well as any Lakeland tarn, being open if not bare. But most folk will tell you it is a black lake. In fact the tarn-name means 'the little black one', from the effect the peaty waters have on its native stock of brown trout which remain small and very dark. The discerning wanderer, with the boots and the will, takes to the fellsides and reaps the rich reward from the discovery of the numerous cairned tops surrounding the lake: Seat How, Rough Crag, Water Crag, Brantrake Crag, Garner Bank, White Pike and the cairnless Rowantree How, visited on the climb to Woodend Height, scenically the best of the bunch. Nonetheless, though set back and hidden from the immediate arena, Yoadcastle must be considered the ultimate goal to the well-rounded expedition.

494 *metres*   1,621 *feet*

ASCENT *from Waberthwaite, Dyke & Broad Oak*

1 Conveniently a small section of old road may be used for parking at the entrance to Dyke Farm. The squat, pepper-pot tower on the hilltop above the farm, connected to Nether Stainton, was erected as a summer-house - *there is no public access*. Follow the farm track through the farm buildings. Rising beyond, watch for the gate left, the bridle-path bears up from the more obvious farm lane. Keep within the walled lane, the pink stonework a quite beautiful construction. Note two combination sheep creeps and shepherds' wall-stiles. A gate spells a change, not one for the better! The next enclosure is traversed by both a bridleway and a footpath. The ground is so rough and *wet*, that horse-riders have been re-directed onto the footpath, making the walkers' lot nigh on impossible, so cling to the wall, hop from tuft to tuft; the fun and games only partially dies down as the path turns right, away from the wall, with the dampest hollow causewayed. On reaching a gate matters improve – *yippee dee!* A clear green way rises easily (passing a chest freezer!), by the obscure remains of the Bronze Age settlement of Barnscar, with traces of field walls and huts lying beneath a dense cover of bracken. The cairned path leads on; a low ridge left, crowned by a cairn, is a spur lure. Crossing wet ground from where a sequence of paired stone markers guide the old path towards the western end of Devoke Water, overlooked by two Bronze Age cairns, the path continuing just above the southern shore.

Harter Fell, Green Crag and Seat How from Devoke Water

Taking the line that most appeals bear off right onto either White Pike, or Stords Hill. Climb onto the subsidiary top of Rowantree How, bound for the great cairn on Woodend Height. **2** White Pike may also be accessed from Broad Oak *(see Stainton Pike chapter page 160)* by climbing onto the Knott, then more steeply to the handsome cairn *(see opposite)*. There is not the slightest hint of a path, you make your own decisions here!

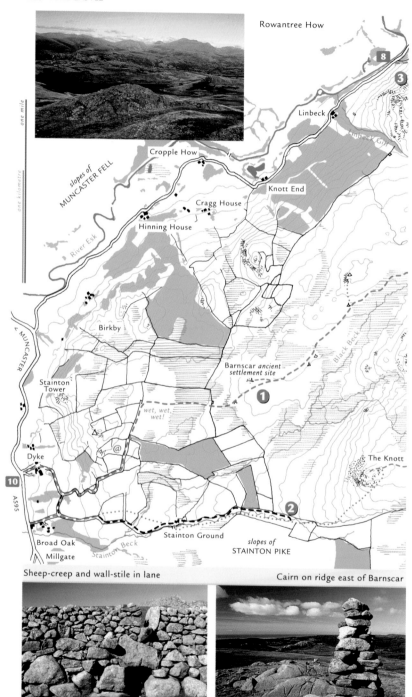

Rowantree How

slopes of
MUNCASTER FELL

River Esk

Cropple How

Linbeck

Knott End

Cragg House

Hinning House

MUNCASTER

Birkby

Stainton
Tower

Barnscar *ancient
settlement site*

1

Black Beck

*wet, wet,
wet!*

Dyke

The Knott

10

A595

2

Broad Oak

Millgate

Stainton Ground

Stainton Beck

slopes of
STAINTON PIKE

8

3

Sheep-creep and wall-stile in lane

Cairn on ridge east of Barnscar

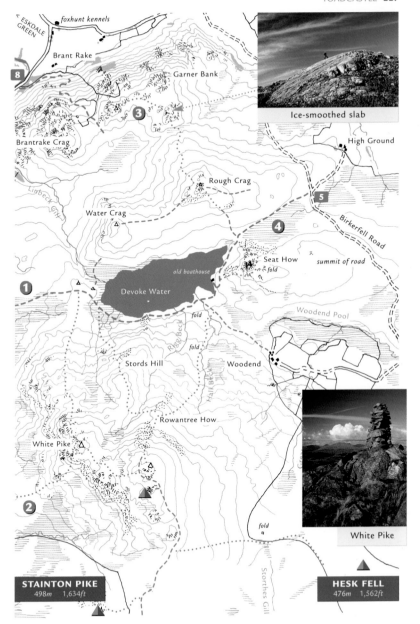

Ice-smoothed slab

ESKDALE GREEN

foxhunt kennels

Brant Rake

8

Garner Bank

Brantrake Crag

High Ground

5

Rough Crag

Water Crag

4

Birkerfell Road

summit of road

Seat How
fold

old boathouse

Devoke Water

1

Woodend Pool

fold

Rigg Beck

fold

Stords Hill

Woodend

Rowantree How

White Pike

2

fold

Storthes Gill

White Pike

STAINTON PIKE
498m   1,634ft

HESK FELL
476m   1,562ft

The fell-name Yoadcastle derives from the Old Norse *jalda* 'a nag or mare' indicating a place of common pasture for horses.

Devoke Water from Woodend Height, backed by a veritable feast of fells

ASCENT *from Brantrake & Birkerfell Road*

3 A small parking area beside the River Esk is a handy springboard. From the hand-gate almost opposite, keep beside the wall under the mightily rough fellside of Brantrake Crag. Coming above the old farm, begin a series of hairpins; the original 'brant rake' or steep steps climbing to a saddle at the old peat sled-gate, typically, dissolves into the combe of Brantrake Moss. Ford the gill left, follow on over the cairned top to the east, traipsing round to a large boiler-plated slab *(see page 234)* composed of a pale rock much in evidence in the vicinity. Head south, slipping through a narrow defile at the head of Hare Gill. Pass a pair of spruces, heading up to the cairn on Rough Crag, a fine viewpoint. Visitors often walk round Devoke Water, taking in the neighbouring cairned top of Water Crag to the west, though the tarn outflowing Linbeck Gill can be deep and troublesome to ford. From Rough Crag descend south east to the boat-house approach track. **4** By parking at the minor junction, on the Birkerfell Road at GR 171977, join the track leading south-west to the tarn, thus avoiding the aforementioned Brantrake section of the ascent. As a novel addition, include Seat How; access to the top is only possible from the east. This rocky knot, commanding a view down the lake, has old enclosure walling on this side too. The track terminates at the ruined Victorian lakeside boat house. A path continues round the southern shore, contending with wet ground. The third beck flowing into the tarn, Rigg Beck is the clue to the ascent. Climb south over Rowantree How onto Woodend Height. There are no paths, symptomatic of all Yoadcastles approaches, though once the high ground is made, there they are... *well, wouldn't you guess it?*

The Summit

On the ground it is clear which is the summit: though maps tend to be a little vague, the whole mass of adjacent ground carrying no distinguishing name. The abrupt summit outcrop is easily mounted. This accesses a small top with only the tiniest of cairns. All effort in that direction has apparently been exhausted in creating Woodend Height's sturdy cairn,

From Barnscar

which is the obvious second port of call, followed by White Pike.

Safe Descents

Be wary of outcropping forming a battlement to White Pike *(see above)*. Otherwise all crags are of a minor nature. While there are no paths off the fell, the gills are universally open-coursed and provide sure guides.

Ridge Route to...

STAINTON PIKE   DESCENT 190*ft*   ASCENT 220*ft*   1.2 miles

A path, little better then a sheep trod *(seen on the chapter title picture)*, leads on a gentle curving line S. Crossing a broad saddle, it mounts a shallow bank from where branch right by a cairn, cross the plain fence to reach the solitary summit cairn – set a little further west than Yoadcastle.

WHITFELL   YOADCASTLE   STAINTON PIKE
Burn Moor
From Woodend Height

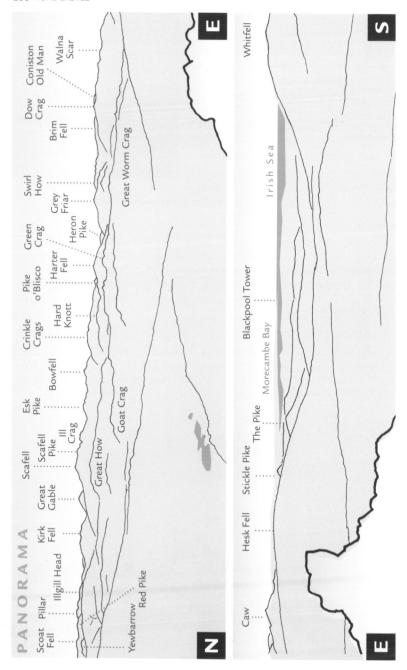

PANORAMA

E

Walna Scar
Coniston Old Man
Dow Crag
Brim Fell
Swirl How
Grey Friar
Green Crag
Heron Pike
Pike o'Blisco
Harter Fell
Crinkle Crags
Hard Knott
Bowfell
Esk Pike
Scafell
Scafell Pike
Ill Crag
Great Gable
Kirk Fell
Illgill Head
Pillar
Scoat Fell

Great Worm Crag
Goat Crag
Great How
Yewbarrow
Red Pike

N

S

Whitfell
Blackpool Tower
The Pike
Stickle Pike
Hesk Fell
Caw

Irish Sea
Morecambe Bay

E

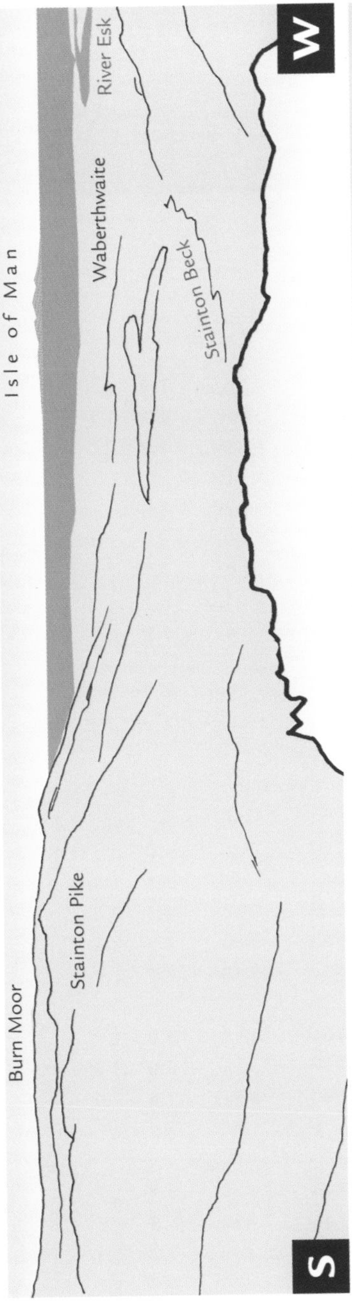

S — W

Isle of Man
River Esk
Waberthwaite
Stainton Beck
Stainton Pike
Burn Moor

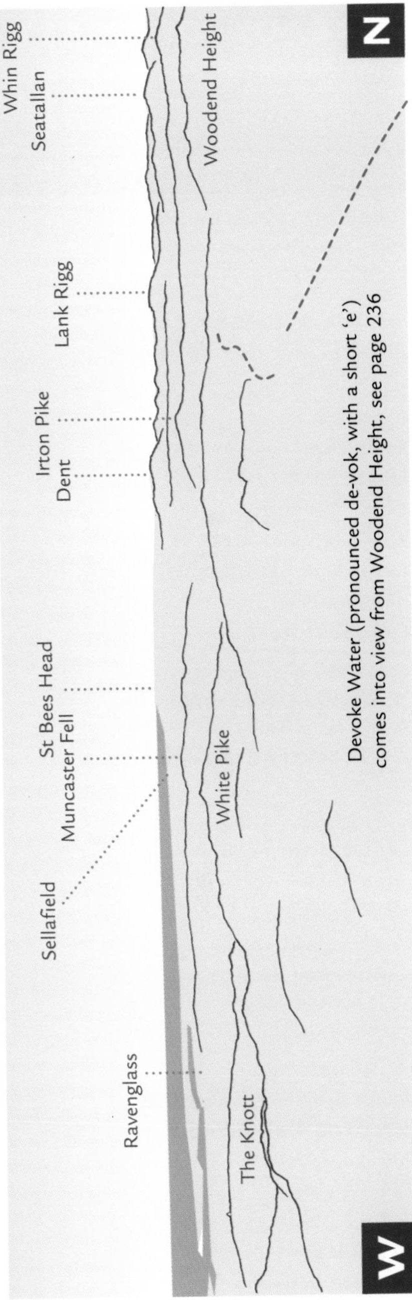

N — W

Whin Rigg
Seatallan
Woodend Height
Lank Rigg
Irton Pike
Dent
St Bees Head
Muncaster Fell
White Pike
Sellafield
Ravenglass
The Knott

Devoke Water (pronounced de-vok, with a short 'e')
comes into view from Woodend Height, see page 236

READY RECKONER *for route-planning*

TO TURN THE FOLLOWING FIGURES INTO WALKING TIME, APPLY NAISMITH'S RULE :

ALLOW **ONE HOUR** FOR EVERY 5km/3 miles
PLUS AN **EXTRA HOUR** FOR EVERY 610m/2,000 feet

WEATHERLINE 017687-75757 24-hour FELL FORECAST

GRADING: **A** *easy route-finding* **B** *some tricky ground* **C** *care in route-finding/mild scrambling*

start & route	text nos.	metres	feet	km	miles	grade
1 Black Combe 14–35						
15 WHITBECK & 16 WHICHAM CHURCH						
via the north ridge	1|2	569	1,865	7.0	4.3	A
to Seaness	3	110	360	2.2	1.4	A
direct ascent	4	565	1,850	3.2	2.0	A
17 BECKSIDE, 18 HALLTHWAITES & 19 CRAGG HALL						
via White Combe	5	555	1,820	5.6	3.5	A
via Whitecombe Beck	6	550	1,805	5.0	3.1	A
via Sty Knotts & Horse Back	7|8	550	1,805	3.2	2.0	A
via Graystones	9	615	2,018	6.7	4.2	A
to Swinside Stone Circle	10	80	262	1.8	1.1	A
14 BOOTLE						
via Old Road	11|12	655	2,150	9.7	5.7	A
via Crookley Beck	11|13|2	605	1,985	6.7	4.2	A
2 Black Fell 36–45						
33 TOM GILL, 34 TARN HOWS – MAIN CAR PARK &						
35 HIGH CROSS – GRISEDALE FOREST						
via Tom Heights & Iron Keld	1|3	224	735	4.0	2.5	A
circuit of Tarn Hows	2	26	85	2.1	1.3	A
via Wharton Tarn	4	158	518	4.5	2.8	A
via Knipe Fold	5	183	600	4.3	2.7	A
via Mountain Road	6	164	540	2.7	1.7	A
36 SILVERTHWAITE & 32 OXEN FELL						
via Low Arnside	7	166	545	3.0	1.9	A
via Park Fell	8	297	975	6.0	3.7	A
descent via Oxen Fell High Cross	9	(61	200)	1.6	1.0	A
3 Brim Fell 46–53						
29 CONISTON & 28 WALNA SCAR ROAD – FELL-GATE						
via Levers Water	1	746	2,450	5.1	1.9	A
via Cove Gill	2	746	2,450	5.3	3.3	B
via Low Water	3	746	2,450	5.3	3.3	B
via Goat's Water	4	570	1,870	4.8	3.0	A

4   Buckbarrow 54-59

13   CORNEYFELL ROAD – ROAD SUMMIT   & 14   BOOTLE

direct	1	150	490	1.8	1.1	A
via the Old Road	2	530	1,740	8.0	5.0	A

12   CORNEYFELL ROAD – BUCKBARROW BRIDGE

via Littlecell Bottom	3	310	1,180	3.5	2.2	A

5   Caw 60-67

46   SEATHWAITE

via Park Head Road	1	425	1,395	2.5	1.6	A
via Green Pikes	2	455	1,490	3.2	2.0	B

25   WATER YEAT BRIDGE – FOREST-GATE   & 23   KILN BANK CROSS

via Lickle Valley	3|4	262	860	4.0	2.5	A
via Long Mire Beck	5	370	1,215	2.2	1.4	B
via Caw Quarry	6	400	1,310	3.7	2.3	A
via Park Head Road	7	320	1,050	3.4	2.1	A

6   Coniston Old Man 68-77

29   CONISTON   & 28   WALNA SCAR ROAD – FELL-GATE

via Church Beck	1	753	2,470	4.2	2.6	A
link to direct route	2	75	250	1.1	0.7	A
via Little Arrow Moor	3	573	2,470	3.2	2.0	A
via The Cove	4	573	2,470	4.0	2.5	B
via Goat's Hause	5	573	2,470	5.4	3.4	A

27   TORVER

via Banishead Quarry	6	695	2,280	5.1	3.2	A

7   Dow Crag 78-87

28   WALNA SCAR ROAD – FELL-GATE

via Walna Scar	1	550	1,800	5.8	3.6	A
via Goat's Hause	2	550	1,800	5.4	3.4	A
via South Rake	3	550	1,800	4.8	3.0	C
via Blind Tarn	4	550	1,800	5.8	3.6	B

27   TORVER

via Banishead Quarry	5	670	2,200	5.9	3.7	A
via Ashgill Quarry	6	675	2,215	6.7	4.2	A

46   SEATHWAITE

via Walna Scar Road	7	680	2,230	6.3	3.9	A
via Seathwaite Tarn	8	680	2,230	8.0	5.0	A

8   Great Carrs 88-95

37   LITTLE LANGDALE   & 39   CASTLE HOW

via Rough Crags	1	668	2,150	6.4	4.0	A
via Greenburn Beck valley	2	686	2,250	6.6	4.1	A
via Swirl Hause/Broad Slack	3	395	1,996	2.2	1.4	B

40   WRYNOSE PASS

via Wrynose Pass	**4**	**395**	1,296	**2.2**	1.4	A

41   WRYNOSE BOTTOM

via Hell Gill	**5**	**523**	1,716	**1.8**	1.2	B

9   Great Worm Crag 96–101

6   BIRKERFELL ROAD – WOODEND BRIDGE *&* 5 DEVOKE WATER

via Freeze Beck	**1|2**	**197**	646	**1.3**	0.8	A
via Birkerthwaite *&* Great Crag	**3**	**217**	712	**2.9**	1.8	A

10   Green Crag 102–109

3   WOOLPACK INN

via Low Birker	**1**	**408**	1,340	**4.0**	2.5	B
via Penny Hill	**2**	**408**	1,340	**4.2**	2.6	B

4   STANLEY GHYLL

via Stanley Force	**3**	**120**	395	**1.9**	1.2	A
via Gate Crag	**4|1**	**352**	1,150	**4.5**	2.8	B

5   BIRKERFELL ROAD – DEVOKE WATER TRACK-END

via Great Crag	**5**	**285**	935	**4.0**	2.5	B

46   SEATHWAITE

via High Wallowbarrow	**6**	**150**	490	**2.2**	1.4	A
via Grassguards	**7|8**	**350**	1,150	**4.3**	2.7	A

11   Grey Friar 110–119

42   COCKLEY BECK BRIDGE *&* 41 WRYNOSE BOTTOM

via Troughton Beck	**1**	**522**	1,710	**2.0**	1.3	A
via Great Intake	**2**	**549**	1,795	**2.4**	1.5	A

44   TROUTAL *&* 45 FICKLE STEPS

via Troutal Fell	**3|7**	**582**	1,910	**4.3**	2.7	A
via Tarn Beck	**4|5|8**	**622**	2,040	**5.4**	3.4	A
via Calf Cove	**6|9**	**662**	2,172	**9.3**	5.8	A

12   Harter Fell 120–129

1   HARDKNOTT PASS

via Demming Crag	**1**	**262**	860	**2.4**	1.5	A

42   COCKLEY BECK BRIDGE, 43 BIRKS BRIDGE *&* 45 FICKLE STEPS

direct	**2**	**466**	1,530	**2.0**	1.3	A
link to Hardknott *ridge*	**3**	**213**	700	**3.2**	2.0	A
valley path to Fickle Steps	**4**	**75**	250	**4.7**	3.0	A
via Grassguards *& forest tracks*	**5|6**	**470**	1,542	**4.0**	2.5	A

2   JUBILEE BRIDGE *&* 3 WOOLPACK INN

via Jubilee Bridge	**7**	**560**	1,837	**3.2**	2.0	A
via Penny Hill	**8**	**580**	1.900	**4.0**	2.5	A
valley path Esk Trail	**9**	**30**	100	**2.6**	1.6	A

13   Hesk Fell 130–137

6   BIRKERFELL ROAD – WOODEND BRIDGE

direct	**1**					A

via Crosbythwaite bridleway	2	**246**	807	**2.0**	1.3	A
21 BOBBIN MILL BRIDGE		**258**	847	**3.2**	2.0	
via Rainsborrow Wood	3|4|6					A
via The Pike & copper mines	3|4|5	**377**	1,237	**5.0**	3.1	A
14 Holme Fell 138–147		**430**	1,410	**3.7**	2.3	
37 LITTLE LANGDALE, 230 TILBERTHWAITE, 31 HODGE CLOSE & 32 OXEN FELL						
via north ridge	2|5					A
via Little Langdale	1|3|4|8	**220**	721	**2.7**	1.7	A
via Low Tilberthwaite	6|7|8	**202**	663	**2.9**	1.8	A
33 TOM GILL		**167**	548	**2.1**	1.3	
via Yew Tree Farm	9					A
15 Muncaster Fell 148–159		**200**	656	**1.4**	0.9	
9 RAVENGLASS & 7 ESKDALE GREEN						
via Walls Castle	1|2					A
via River Esk	3|4	**230**	755	**4.0**	2.5	A
via Muncaster Mill	5	**233**	765	**5.5**	3.4	A
via Fell Lane	6	**76**	250	**1.0**	0.6	A
via Irton Road & The Green	7|8|9|10	**150**	492	**1.6**	1.0	A
valley path High Eskholme	11	**192**	630	**3.8**	2.4	A
16 Stainton Pike 160–167		**130**	427	**3.7**	2.3	
11 WABERTHWAITE – BROAD OAK						
via Rowantree Force	1					A
via Stainton Ground	2	**393**	1,290	**4.2**	2.6	A
17 Stickle Pike 168–175		**470**	1,542	**3.8**	2.4	
23 KILN BANK CROSS						
direct	1|2					A
24 BROUGHTON MILLS		**117**	384	**0.5**	0.3	
traverse of the Fox Haw ridge	3					A
via Hare Hall	4	**400**	1,312	**3.2**	2.0	A
via Great Stickle	5	**368**	1,207	**2.7**	1.7	A
22 ULPHA		**405**	1,330	**3.0**	1.9	
via Tarn Hill	6					A
via Low Birks	7	**358**	1,175	**2.9**	1.8	A
18 Swirl How 176–183		**308**	1,010	**2.4**	1.5	
29 CONISTON & 28 WALNA SCAR ROAD – FELL-GATE						
via Levers Hause	1|2	**744**	2,440	**4.8**	3.0	A
via Swirl Hause	3	**744**	2,440	**4.6**	2.9	A
37 LITTLE LANGDALE & 40 WRYNOSE PASS						
via Greenburn Beck valley	4	**680**	2,230	**5.1**	3.2	A
via Rough Crags	5	**685**	2,247	**5.8**	3.6	A
via Wet Side Edge	6	**411**	1,348	**2.6**	1.6	A

19 Wallowbarrow Crag 184-189

46 SEATHWAITE

via Wallowbarrow Gorge	1|2|3|4	232	761	**3.8** 2.4	A
via High Wallowbarrow	5	187	614	**1.0** 0.6	A

20 Walna Scar 190-199

28 WALNA SCAR ROAD – FELL-GATE

via Walna Scar Road	1	390	1,280	**3.2** 2.0	A

26 HUMMER LANE

via Bleaberry Haws	2	500	1,640	**4.1** 2.6	B

25 WATER YEAT BRIDGE – FOREST-GATE

via River Lickle	3	460	1,510	**3.8** 2.4	A
via Broughton Forest	4	100	280	**2.9** 1.8	A
via Walna Scar Quarry	5	444	1,457	**4.0** 2.5	A

46 SEATHWAITE

via Walna Scar Road	6	520	1,706	**3.5** 2.2	A
via Gobling Beck	7	520	1,706	**3.8** 2.4	A

21 Wetherlam 200-215

29 CONISTON

via Sweeten Crag & Lad Stones	1|2|3|4	730	2,395	**5.3** 3.3	A
via Red Dell & Black Sails	5|6	715	2,346	**6.4** 4.0	A
via Swirl Hause	7	715	2,346	**7.0** 4.4	A
via Yewdale Fells	8|9|10				A

30 TILBERTHWAITE3, 7 LITTLE LANGDALE & 38 CATHEDRAL QUARRY

via Steel Edge & Birkfell Hause	11|12|13	640	2,100	**3.4** 2.1	B
via Low Fell	14	720	2,362	**5.0** 3.1	B
via Greenburn MIne	15|16	662	2,172	**5.1** 3.2	A
via Swirl Hause	17|18	660	2,165	**6.9** 4.3	A

22 Whitfell 216-223

20 BRACKENTHWAITE

via Bigert Pasture	1	373	1,224	**3.8** 2.4	A

12 CORNEYFELL ROAD – BUCKBARROW BRIDGE & 11 FELL LANE

via Burn Moor	2	353	1,158	**4.5** 2.8	A
via Fell Lane	3|4	473	1,552	**5.1** 3.2	A

23 Yoadcastle 224-231

11 CORNEYFELL ROAD – FELL LANE & 10 DYKE

via Barnscar	1	472	1,550	**7.2** 4.5	A
via Stainton Beck	2	468	1,535	**5.3** 3.3	A

8 BRANTRAKE & 5 BIRKERFELL ROAD – DEVOKE WATER TRACK-END

via Rough Crag & Seat How	3	560	1,837	**5.9** 3.7	A
via Devoke Water	4	256	840	**3.7** 2.3	A

FELL FILE

Mark up your fells

NEAR EASTERN FELLS

ARNISON CRAG
434m 1,424ft   *NY 393149*

BIRKHOUSE MOOR
718m 2,356ft   *NY 365164*

BIRKS
622m 2,241ft   *NY 382144*

CATSTYCAM
890m 2,920ft   *NY 348158*

CLOUGH HEAD
726m 2,386ft   *NY 334226*

DOLLYWAGGON PIKE
858m 2,815ft   *NY 336131*

DOVE CRAG
792m 2,599ft   *NY 374104*

FAIRFIELD
873m 2,864ft   *NY 359117*

GLENRIDDING DODD
442m 1,450ft   *NY 381176*

GOWBARROW FELL
481m 1,578ft   *NY 407218*

GREAT DODD
857m 2,812ft   *NY 342205*

GREAT MELL FELL
537m 1,762ft   *NY 397254*

GREAT RIGG
767m 2,516ft   *NY 355104*

HART CRAG
822m 2,697ft   *NY 369112*

HART SIDE
758m 2,487ft   *NY 359197*

HARTSOP ABOVE HOW
586m 1,923ft   *NY 384121*

HELVELLYN
950m 3,116ft   *NY 332152*

HERON PIKE
621m 2,037ft   *NY 356082*

HIGH HARTSOP DODD
619m 1,703ft   *NY 394107*

HIGH PIKE
612m 2,152ft   *NY 374088*

LITTLE MELL FELL
505m 1,657ft   *NY 423240*

LITTLE HART CRAG
637m 2,090ft   *NY 387100*

LOW PIKE
507m 1,663ft   *NY 373078*

MIDDLE DODD
653m 2,143ft   *NY 397096*

NETHERMOST PIKE
891m 2,923ft   *NY 344141*

NAB SCAR
455m 1,490ft   *NY 355073*

RAISE
884m 2,900ft   *NY 343174*

RED SCREES
777m 2,549ft   *NY 396087*

SEAT SANDAL
736m 2,415ft   *NY 343115*

SHEFFIELD PIKE
675m 2,215ft   *NY 369182*

ST SUNDAY CRAG
841m 2,759ft   *NY 369134*

STONE ARTHUR
503m 1,650ft   *NY 347092*

STYBARROW DODD
846m 2,776ft   *NY 343189*

WATSON'S DODD
789m 2,589ft   *NY 336195*

WHITE SIDE
863m 2,851ft   *NY 338166*

CENTRAL FELLS

ARMBOTH FELL
479m 1,572ft   NY 296157

BELL CRAGS
558m 1,831ft   NY 298143

BLEABERRY FELL
589m 1,932ft   NY 286196

BLEA RIGG
556m 1,824ft   NY 298079

CALF CRAG
537m 1,762ft   NY 302104

EAGLE CRAG
520m 1,706ft   NY 275121

GIBSON KNOTT
421m 1,380ft   NY 318099

GRANGE FELL
416m 1,365ft   NY 265163

GREAT CRAG
452m 1,483ft   NY 270146

HARRISON STICKLE
736m 2,415ft   NY 282074

HELM CRAG
405m 1,329ft   NY 327093

HIGH RAISE
762m 2,500ft   NY 281095

HIGH RIGG
355m 1,165ft   NY 308220

HIGH SEAT
608m 1,995ft   NY 287181

HIGH TOVE
515m 1,690ft   NY 289165

LOFT CRAG
692m 2,270ft   NY 298071

LOUGHRIGG FELL
335m 1,099ft   NY 348052

PAVEY ARK
697m 2,288ft   NY 285079

PIKE O'STICKLE
708m 2,323ft   NY 274074

RAVEN CRAG
463m 1,519ft   NY 303187

SERGEANT MAN
736m 2,414ft   NY 286099

SERGEANT'S CRAG
574m 1,883ft   NY 274114

SILVER HOW
395m 1,296ft   NY 325066

STEEL FELL
553m 1,814ft   NY 319112

TARN CRAG
485m 1,591ft   NY 303093

THUNACAR KNOTT
723m 2,372ft   NY 279080

ULLSCARF
726m 2,382ft   NY 292122

WALLA CRAG
379m 1,243ft   NY 277213

MID-WESTERN FELLS

ALLEN CRAGS
784m 2,572ft   NY 236085

BOWFELL
903m 2,963ft   NY 244064

COLD PIKE
701m 2,300ft   NY 263036

CRINKLE CRAGS
860m 2,822ft   NY 250054

ESKDALE MOOR
337m 1,105ft   NY 177034

ESK PIKE
885m 2,904ft   NY 237075

GLARAMARA
783m 2,569ft   NY 246104

GREAT END
907m 2,976ft   NY 225085